THE BOOK
of the
YEAR

Special Days and their Meanings

R. BRASCH

Illustrated by
MAXIM SVETLANOV

Angus&Robertson
An imprint of HarperCollins*Publishers*

AN ANGUS & ROBERTSON BOOK
An imprint of HarperCollinsPublishers

First published in Australia in 1991
Reprinted in 1991, 1992, 1993

CollinsAngus&Robertson Publishers Pty Limited
A division of HarperCollinsPublishers (Australia) Pty Limited
25 Ryde Road, Pymble NSW 2073, Australia

HarperCollinsPublishers (New Zealand) Limited
31 View Road, Glenfield, Auckland 10, New Zealand

HarperCollinsPublishers Limited
77–85 Fulham Palace Road, London W6 8JB, United Kingdom

Copyright © R. Brasch 1991
Illustrations copyright © M. Svetlanov 1991

National Library of Australia
Cataloguing-in-Publication data:

Brasch, R. (Rudolph), 1912 –
 The book of the year
 Includes index.
 ISBN 0 207 16656 0.
 1. Days. 2. Months. I. Title.
398.236

Illustrated by Maxim Svetlanov
Typeset in Bernhard Modern
Printed in Singapore

7 6 5 4
96 95 94 93

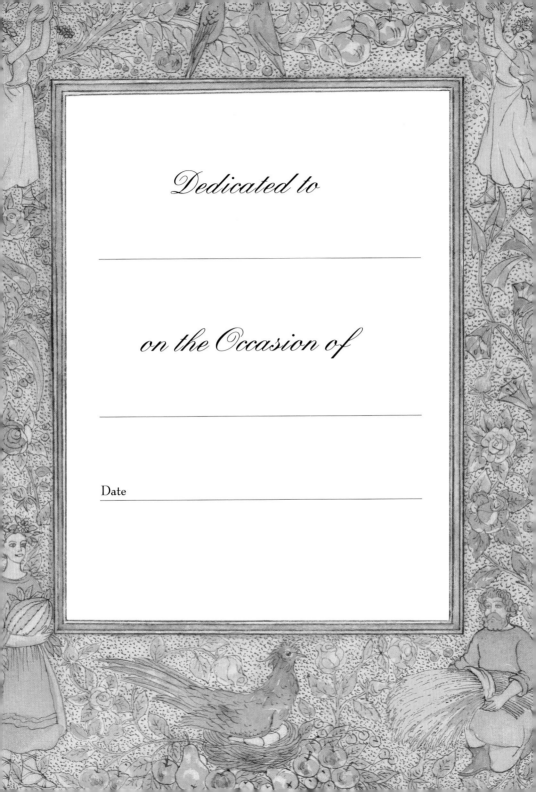

Dedicated to

_____

on the Occasion of

_____

Date _____

Our Family's Special Dates

MOMENTS AND EVENTS TO BE REMEMBERED

_____

_____

_____

_____

_____

_____

_____

_____

_____

_____

CONTENTS

Preface

The Book of the Year is a perpetual calendar of special days and their meanings. It deals with the festivals, feast days and red-letter days throughout the entire year and the customs associated with them. It tells how they all started and why they are significant, and explores the meaning and relevance of their celebrations and sometimes puzzling practices. It ranges from the secular to the religious and from personal celebrations to national and international holidays and contains a wealth of fascinating facts and legends.

Most of the days and celebrations are listed and explained in the order in which they occur in the calendar. Feasts such as Easter and the Jewish festivals which, traditionally, are held according to the lunar calendar and therefore have a different date every year, have been placed in this book in the month in which they most commonly occur. Individual chapters deal with major feasts of the Muslim, Hindu and Buddhist faiths and with festival days celebrated by the Chinese and the Japanese people.

An understanding of these festivals and celebrations enhances our appreciation of traditions to which we are heir. Kipling once said that to appreciate one's own country fully one has to go abroad. This applies equally to customs and traditions; to understand our own we need to learn about those of other nations and cultures.

It is customary for authors to dedicate any work they write to someone special. To make this Book of the Year something truly intimate, the spot usually reserved for a dedication is left empty. It is there waiting for you to fill it, and there is space for you to add an appropriate thought or message.

The Calendar Year

January

January is called after Janus, the Roman god of gateways and beginnings. His name is derived from the Latin ianua, meaning 'door'. Always represented with two faces, simultaneously surveying the past and looking into the future, Janus was a most fitting choice to have the opening month of the year dedicated to him.

New Year's Day

*N*ew Year's Day is man's oldest holiday. It has been universally celebrated on many different dates and in the most varied ways.

The Romans were the first to celebrate it on 1 January — in 153 BC. Until then they had started the new year on 25 March, chosen because the date coincided with the time of the vernal equinox, when day and night were of equal length. The new date no longer had any connection with the cycle of nature. It had a political significance, being the date on which the newly elected Roman consuls assumed office.

Christians, at first, strongly rejected the celebration of New Year on 1 January as a pagan institution. Eventually, however, they welcomed it by changing it into a religious festival. It commemorated Jesus' circumcision. Like any other Jewish boy, he had been initiated into the Covenant of Abraham on the eighth day after his birth, which was 1 January.

It was a long time before Europeans generally began to adopt 1 January as New Year's Day. As a result of Pope Gregory XIII's calendar reform in 1582, Catholic countries were the first to adopt it. Protestant Europe followed later. England and Wales (and Britain's American colonies) did not celebrate New Year on 1 January until 1752!

Whenever it fell, New Year was, from the very beginning, a

significant day. It symbolised the renewal of life and human relationships. Quarrels were made up and everything was done to make it a memorable and festive occasion.

Customs Observed

New Year's traditions were not based on the pursuit of mere fun and jollification. Their purpose was to wipe out the evils of the past and to ensure a new start. Moreover, anything that happened or that was done on the day, or on its eve, assumed a 'fateful' meaning. It would affect the rest of the year. Carefully and anxiously, then, people were concerned about what they did and whom they met, whether inside or outside the house.

Nothing should be taken out of one's home on the day because one might easily remove one's good luck along with it. Instead, it was wise to make sure that lots of things were carried in. As well, both one's pockets and one's stomach should be full. This would make certain that in the ensuing year one would be prosperous and well fed. Empty pockets and unstocked shelves or cupboards augured a year of poverty.

The variety of New Year's customs in different regions and countries is almost unlimited. In one canton of Switzerland, for instance, it was the practice, despite Swiss people's traditional and fastidious cleanliness, to spill some cream onto the floor. It would bring a year of overflowing abundance.

The 'First Footer'

The most famous New Year custom is 'first footing'. It originated in Scotland and is still observed. It goes back to the old tradition that whoever first 'set foot' into a home after the new year had started decided the family's luck for the rest of the year. This is based on man's early belief in the magic power of beginnings. The start of the new year controlled its future course.

Most welcome as a 'first footer' was a tall, dark-haired man, especially if he carried a gift. He was a harbinger of good things to come. Magically, his handsome features would make the year a pleasant one and his gift of an essential item — such as a loaf of bread or, in earlier days, a shovel of coal — would ensure that there would be no lack of food or warmth in the house.

A woman, anyone fair-haired or, worst of all, a man who was short and cross-eyed, would prove disastrous, presaging bad days to come. It was not surprising, therefore, that people sometimes subtly arranged for the right kind of visitor to arrive.

New Year Gifts

Before they became practical in nature, New Year presents had a magic significance. Thus, the gift of branches from sacred trees was believed to bring the gods' blessings into the home. Druids chose twigs from the mistletoe, a plant sacred to them as a magic source of fertility. It would bestow on the recipient a fruitful year: in the number

of his children, as well as of his cattle, and in the size of his crop.

Gloves later became a traditional New Year present in England; they were most useful in winter. This explains why monetary gifts, which eventually took their place, were referred to as 'glove money'. Before the invention of buttons, pins were in great demand. As they were often in short supply, they were considered precious and were, for some time, a welcome New Year gift.

With the passing of time, necessities, values and beliefs changed and, with them, the kinds of presents that were traditionally given at New Year.

Wishes and Resolutions

Wishes for a 'Happy New Year' accompanied the gifts one sent. They can be traced far back into antiquity and were found — a forerunner of the modern New Year card — in Egyptian tombs!

Medals specially struck during Hadrian's reign (in the second century) expressed, on behalf of the senate and people of Rome, wishes for the emperor, 'the father of the country', for a 'Happy and Prosperous New Year'.

Of all the greeting cards known to celebrate the rites of passage', those sent for New Year certainly are the oldest ones. Well known is a sixteenth-century woodcut, which was very popular at the time. It shows the Christ child with a cart loaded with a bag of good wishes, arriving at a home. On being questioned by the gatekeeper as to his identity and mission, the child replies, 'It is I, bringing a good year'.

As well as wishing each other a happy and prosperous New Year,

it became customary for people to make personal New Year's resolutions. If carried out, they would become further cause for celebration.

1 JANUARY

The Horses' Birthday

he first of January is the official birthday of all horses. Irrespective of when a horse was actually born, its birth will be celebrated on this day and, much more significantly, its age will be calculated accordingly. No matter how old it really is, on the 1 January after its birth the horse ceases to be a weanling and becomes a yearling.

The date was not chosen arbitrarily. It is related to the breeding season and was selected to give the horse its best chance when competing in races in its age group. A horse that is foaled soon after 1 January has the longest time to grow big and strong before it is classed a yearling.

In Australia, where the seasons differ from those of the northern hemisphere, 1 August has been designated as the horses' birthday.

5–6 JANUARY

Twelfth Night and Twelfth Day

he 'Twelfth Day' after Christmas, better known by the celebration of its eve, 'Twelfth Night', concludes the festive season.

As a last opportunity for revelry before they returned to their daily work, people used to spend the night exuberantly, with games, disguises and plays. Among the comedies often performed was Shakespeare's *Twelfth Night,* specifically written and fittingly named for the occasion.

The revelry of former days is no longer practised. However, as the 'Twelfth Day' marks the end of the Christmas season, it is still traditional to leave Christmas decorations in place until then.

6 JANUARY

The Three Magi and the Feast of the Epiphany

On 6 January Christians observed the Feast of the Epiphany, as on this day the Magi, the three wise men from the East, are said to have arrived at Bethlehem with their gifts for the infant Jesus.

It was the first time that he was shown to the Gentile world, and it is this 'manifestation' which is commemorated on the Feast of the Epiphany. Its name comes from the Greek epiphany, which means 'manifestation' or 'showing'.

It is popularly believed that the three Magi, following a star, came to pay homage to the baby Jesus. The Gospels' account, the original source of the story, gives no indication of the names, or the number, of the visitors; nor does it say, as is often claimed, that they were kings.

These fanciful details were added much later. Tertullian, who was

converted to Christianity in AD 190 and who became a famous Father of the Church, was the first to suggest that the Magi were *'almost kings'* (he used the Latin words *fere reges*). It was at least another 300 years before the Magi's royal status was taken for granted. The visit was claimed to have been anticipated by the Psalmist who had spoken (in Psalm 72:10) of far-off kings who 'shall bring presents' and 'offer gifts'.

Origen, a third-century Father of the Church and eminent biblical scholar, was the first to assert that they were three in number. It was indicated in the Gospels, he wrote, by the three different gifts they carried — the gold, the frankincense and the myrrh. The claim that their names were Gaspar, Melchior and Balthasar is of even later date.

15 JANUARY

Martin Luther King's Birthday

An American national holiday now — and the most recently proclaimed of all — is the anniversary of Martin Luther King's birthday (in 1929). It honours the man whose fight against racial discrimination and for civil rights, and whose assassination at the young age of thirty-nine rocked the American nation to its very foundation. King was killed on 4 April 1968 in Memphis, where he had gone to support a garbage workers' strike.

His 'dream' of the day when his (black) people, and indeed all people, would be judged by their character, and not by the colour of their skin, became an inspiration all over the world. His leadership in

the civil rights movement and his belief in non-violence as the best means of obtaining equal justice, gained him the Nobel Peace Prize in 1964. Only thirty-five years old at the time, he was the youngest person ever to be given this award.

King is the first, and so far the only, black person in the United States to be honoured by a public holiday and only the second American — George Washington was the first — to have a special day set aside in his memory.

Commemorations of King's birthday centre on the inspirational 'I have a dream' speech, which he gave at the 1963 march on Washington. Bells are tolled in all fifty states, and ceremonies also include the symbolic tapping of the Liberty Bell and the actual ringing of the Independence Bell in Philadelphia. An ever-increasing number of other countries join in the celebration in which King's philosophy, as well as its contemporary meaning and application, is expounded. His birthday has become a 'day for peace and non-violence'.

20 JANUARY

Inauguration Day

The United States presidential election is held every four years, and the 20 January following this is Inauguration Day. It is the date on which the President, sworn in by the Chief Justice of the Supreme Court, assumes office. The date used to vary and it was only in 1933 that, by the Twentieth Amendment to the Constitution, Congress finally fixed it.

George Washington, the first President of the United States, was

inaugurated in New York City, which was the temporary capital, on 30 April 1789. Thomas Jefferson's inauguration, the first to be held in Washington D.C., was conducted on 4 March 1801.

The Founding Fathers envisaged the day as one of simple ceremony, centring on the administration of the oath, in which the new President promised faithfully to execute his office and 'to the best of my ability [to] preserve, protect and defend the Constitution of the United States'. With the passing of the years (and of presidents), Inauguration Day grew into an ever more elaborate and festive occasion. Its program came to include a gala ball, military parades and other colourful celebrations watched by thousands. Its most significant feature, however, became and remains the President's inaugural address.

Memorable phrases distinguish some of the speeches delivered on the occasion. They may reflect the special historic circumstances of the time or be indicative of the stature of the president. Abraham Lincoln, who had experienced the tragic destruction and loss of life brought about by the Civil War, solemnly promised to 'finish the work we are in [and] to bind up the nation's wounds'. It was in his inaugural address, given at the very depth of the Great Depression in 1933, that Franklin D. Roosevelt first made the observation — so often quoted since — that 'the only thing we have to fear is fear itself'. Many a statesman has repeated the message John F. Kennedy gave on the occasion of his inauguration: 'Ask not what your country can do for you — ask what you can do for your country'.

The Odd Story of any Inauguration

Inauguration as a term can be traced to ancient Roman augury! The function of an officially appointed soothsayer was to observe the flight of birds and, by interpreting it, to select 'auspicious' days on which to hold events of national importance or to embark on significant ventures.

The etymology of the words recalls their 'bird-watching' origin. 'Auspicious' joins *avis* ('bird' in Latin) with *specio* (which means 'I observe'). 'Inauguration' combines the Latin *augur* (which preceded *avis* as the word for 'bird') and the verb *garrio* (which means 'I talk' or 'I chatter'). No doubt, it referred to the soothsayer's ability to understand the message contained in the mystifying but meaningful sounds made by the birds.

The application of the ancient meanings to the modern institution would suggest that Inauguration Day should be the most propitious day for a new President to assume his term of office.

26 JANUARY
Australia Day

Australia Day commemorates the landing of Captain Arthur Phillip and the convicts of the First Fleet in 1788 at what is now called Sydney Cove. The establishment of the first British settlement on Australian soil was the starting point for the building of a modern nation in the ancient land.

Previously, Britain had sent her convicts to America which, after gaining independence, refused to accept any further transportees. Far-off Australia was chosen as the most suitable alternative. Paradoxically, the day of the arrival of the first of these convicts has become a national holiday and an occasion of celebration.

Until quite recently, whenever 26 January fell midweek, the celebration was moved to the following Monday. This practice satisfied the typically Australian love of the 'long weekend'. However, there were strong objections to this custom. It was felt that, regardless of when in the week the day occurs, as a day of national pride and unity, its historical associations should take precedence over mere hedonistic concerns.

Another problem which has been highlighted in recent times is that while the day commemorates European settlement, it totally ignores the Aborigines who have populated the continent for thousands of years. Many Aborigines regard Australia Day not as a day of pride, but as one of shame — a commemoration of white man's invasion of their land.

The Chinese New Year

Though modern China has adopted the Gregorian solar calendar and hence, officially, begins the New Year on 1 January, it continues to celebrate the traditional Chinese lunar year, which has been renamed the Spring Festival. It falls on the first new moon after

the sun has entered the constellation of Aquarius, which may be any time in late January or early February.

The most popular features in the celebrations are the lion and dragon dances. Youths don strange and bizarre disguises, made of different types of cloth, to represent and operate the animal bodies. With monstrous head and often breathing fire, dragons weave through the streets, which are ablaze with lights. To the amusement of the crowds of onlookers, they wriggle in grotesque patterns, imitating and exaggerating the movements of living creatures.

Now enjoyed as pure entertainment, the dragons and lions recall totems that were worshipped in former times. The dance survives from an ancient magic rite of exorcism. It was practised to drive away the evil spirits that threatened the rebirth of nature and, therefore, people's wealth and prosperity.

The dragons, indeed, merit a special place in the festivities of the day. Though they are supernatural beings, they also symbolised the reproductive energies of nature. Fearsome in appearance, they were renowned for their vigilance, and were therefore welcomed as protectors. They would guard the people and the nation throughout the year which was about to begin.

The celebration of the New Year, which may extend well over three days, is observed by family reunions, with sumptuous banquets and special dishes, and visits to friends. It is a time of renewal of all bonds. It is also an occasion of general reconciliation when quarrels of the past must be forgotten and all debts settled. In fact, it is considered unlucky to start the New Year with unpaid accounts.

Ancient customs and superstitions, though now rationalised, are still conscientiously carried out. They include the thorough spring

cleaning of the house in preparation for the day. Originally carried out to sweep away all past misfortune, it is now explained as a hygienic measure. All damage is repaired and the home repainted to symbolise the renewal of life.

Tradition demands that no knives, scissors or other cutting implements be used at home on New Year. To use them could result in the magical severing of precious links. Accordingly, all food is prepared on the preceding days.

Presents are thoughtfully chosen, not only for their usefulness but also for their symbolism. Chinese tradition requires that the recipient returns at least a portion of the gift, thereby expressing his unworthiness to receive it.

The day's festive atmosphere is further enhanced by the decoration of homes and streets with yellow-tasselled lanterns, by the letting off of fireworks and the explosion of countless crackers which, by their noise, are believed to frighten away the evil spirits. Red, the colour of good omens and happiness, predominates everywhere. Streamers embellish the streets and houses. People wish each other wealth and prosperity in the year ahead, success in all undertakings and a long line of descendants — 'ten thousand generations', according to the ancient formula.

The Animals in the Chinese Calendar

*E*ach year has its individual name, called after one of the twelve animals that make up the Chinese zodiac.

A fable about an event in Buddha's life explains their choice. He had extended an invitation to all living creatures, but only twelve of them answered his call. They were the Rat, the Ox, the Tiger, the Rabbit, the Dragon, the Snake, the Horse, the Sheep, the Monkey, the Rooster, the Dog and the Pig. As a reward, Buddha commemorated their visit by naming a year after each of them.

The sequence of the years, so a legend tells, was determined by a cross-country race between these very animals, and is the order in which they reached the finish.

February

*F*ebruary means 'purification' — from the Latin
februare. It derives its name from an ancient fertility
rite, which was part of a Roman festival celebrated during
this month.

Its ceremonial took a peculiar form. Youths were provided
with thongs cut from the hides of sacrificed goats — animals
reputed for their virility and fecundity. Thus equipped, they ran
through the streets of Rome, seeking out women known to have
proved barren and whose infertility was thought to be the result
of some 'uncleanliness'. By whipping them with their thongs,
so it was believed, the youths 'purified' the women's bodies
which, thus cleansed, would be able to conceive.

Waitangi Day:

New Zealand's National Day

*N*ew Zealand's national day is unique of its kind. Known as Waitangi Day, it is named after the town on the Bay of Islands where, in 1840, a treaty was signed by the English settlers — represented by Captain William Hobson, who was later to become the first Governor of New Zealand — and some fifty Maori chiefs on behalf of their nation. The Treaty of Waitangi decreed that, henceforth, both peoples would live in peace! Missionaries and officials then took the document to other parts of the country, giving more Maories, mainly chiefs, an opportunity to add their marks. Eventually, thus, the treaty contained 512 signatures.

St Valentine's Day

*S*t Valentine's Day, on 14 February, is a day of romance and love on which we send anonymous messages or cards that express our affection to those for whom we care deeply. Once, such Valentine cards were individually written. Nowadays, like Christmas cards, they can be purchased ready-made.

The celebration of this day goes back thousands of years, to ancient Rome. Falling during the season of spring, it was considered a time particularly propitious for love. It was believed that birds started

to mate on this day and that, therefore, it would be only natural for humans to pair off as well.

The fourteenth of February became the lovers' festival. Known as Lupercalia it was dedicated to the Roman goddess Juno, who was worshipped as the guardian of women and marriage. Special lotteries were held in her honour. The prizes to be won were not valuable objects or sums of money, but lovers. Girls wrote their names on slips of paper. These they placed into a large drum, from which the young men drew their 'lot'. There were no blanks. The girls thus 'allotted' became the ticket holder's sweetheart until the next draw, held in the following year, once again on Juno's feast.

Christians tried hard to uproot the pagan festival. Failing to do so, they renamed Juno's feast, calling it after Valentine, one of the Christian saints. The choice was the result of a peculiar coincidence of dates.

The Roman Emperor Claudius believed that husbands did not make good soldiers. Anxious to get back to their wives, they easily neglected their martial duties. For this reason he decided to abolish the institution of marriage and, with utmost rigour, tried to enforce his policy.

Valentine, who was a Roman bishop at the time, felt that the edict contradicted the will of God and was against human nature. He therefore continued — though now secretly — to marry young lovers. But he could not do so for long. His clandestine solemnisations were discovered. Arrested, he was thrown into prison, scourged and eventually beheaded in AD 269. It is supposed that he suffered martyrdom on 14 February, the very day dedicated to Juno. Ever since, it was kept as St Valentine's Day and was considered, even by

the Church, a date most appropriate for declarations of love.

Tradition tells that, while in prison, Valentine had fallen in love with the gaoler's daughter, whose blindness he had miraculously cured. In a letter he declared his passionate feelings towards her, signing it 'From your Valentine'. And it was his signature that gave us the Valentine card!

However successful the Church had been in substituting the pagan feast with St Valentine's Day, it was unable to wean the people from the lottery of love. So it altered the prizes! It replaced the girls' names by those of saints. Now the 'lucky' winner was expected in the ensuing year to match his life to that of the saint whose name he had drawn. The scheme misfired. No one liked the new type of lottery. In no time, girls regained possession of the drum and the ancient love play resumed.

It was not to last, however. People came to resent the practice of having their sweethearts chosen for them — by chance. They felt that their own choice should take the place of luck. On 14 February they thus began to send cards, sets of verses or even gifts to the ones they admired. They often did so anonymously, and it was left to the recipient to guess the author or donor. Those unable to find their own words selected them from special handbooks, published for the purpose. Some of these, such as *The Young Man's Valentine Writer*, date back to 1797.

Eventually, the printed Valentine card came into existence. The introduction of cheap postal rates added greatly to their popularity, already assured by the intriguing mystery of the unnamed sender's identity.

Presidents' Day

The American people felt that just as the English celebrated their monarch's birthday, the Republic should make the birthday of its President a public holiday as well. Thus, George Washington's birthday — 22 February — became an occasion of festivity, even during his lifetime. It was then decided that Abraham Lincoln's date of birth — 12 February — should equally be honoured. Both men had been greatly admired for the part they played in building up the American nation and their lives had become legends.

For many years, therefore, their birthdays were commemorated as national holidays. It was then felt that it would be much more practical to combine their individual celebrations and to remember both men on one day. This created Presidents' Day.

Fixed for the third Monday in February, the date was particularly chosen because of its close proximity to the birth of Washington, thereby paying special tribute to the Republic's foundation President.

By no longer identifying a specific head of state, Presidents' Day now honours not merely the two renowned men, as originally intended, but each and every President of the past, the present and the future.

Leap Year Proposals

Long before women's liberation, spinsters were given equal rights with men — but only every fourth year, and then exclusively in the realm of marriage! They were permitted to propose to men during

leap years. There are several explanations of the origin of this tradition.

It was once believed — though this has since been proved untrue — that in 1288 Queen Margaret of Scotland had given women this right. Any man who refused to accept such a proposal could be fined a hundred pounds. Bachelors were quick to appreciate the threat and soon took precautionary measures. Though forced to recognise and submit to the women's newly achieved right to 'pop the question' during leap years, they restricted it by stipulating that a woman could do so only if she wore a clearly visible red petticoat. This gave the men due warning — and the opportunity to take evasive action!

Another legend links the introduction of leap year proposals with two well-known saints, at a time when celibacy was not compulsory for priests and nuns. It tells how St Bridget called on St Patrick to ask his advice. The nuns in her charge, she told him, had become very restive. They objected to the man having the sole right to propose marriage. Why should women not be equally entitled to take the initiative?

Patrick fully understood the problem. To pacify the nuns, he suggested a compromise solution. Henceforth women would be allowed to propose; they could do so for a full year — every seventh year! Though not entirely satisfied, Bridget expressed her appreciation by throwing her arms around Patrick who, no doubt, must have enjoyed her show of affection. His pleasure did not go unnoticed and Bridget, grasping the opportunity, now implored Patrick to extend the right by making it valid every fourth year. In the circumstances, he could not resist her plea. In fact, he agreed to make it not only every fourth year, but the longest year in every four — which, of course, was leap year!

The Season of Lent

ent is the period of forty days before Easter. As the date of Easter, determined by the first full moon after the vernal equinox, changes from year to year, the beginning of Lent varies accordingly and may fall either in February or March.

The name Lent merely reflects the seasonal fact that at this time of the year, in the northern hemisphere, the days noticeably begin to 'lengthen' (*lenctene* in Old English). That Lent extends over forty days commemorates the forty days Jesus spent fasting in the wilderness before embarking on his ministry. Accordingly, it is a solemn season. In the early days of the Church people abstained totally from eating meat, eggs, milk, butter or fat, and from having any sexual relations. In addition, they were expected to avoid any other food of which they were specially fond. The prohibition of sex survives in the superstition that it is unlucky to get married during Lent.

Certain days associated with Lent — occurring either before or during it — have their own particular features.

Shrove Tuesday

Shrove Tuesday is the last day before the long fast of Lent. Its name recalls how on this day the faithful confessed their sins and did penance for them. This act of 'confession and absolution' used to be referred to in archaic English as 'being shriven' — hence the 'Shrove' in Shrove Tuesday.

Being sorry for one's sins, however, was only part of what the day was all about. Shrove Tuesday had a very joyful side as well, as is evidenced by the variety of other names, among them Pancake Tuesday, Carnival and Mardi Gras, by which it is known. Each has its own story.

Pancake Tuesday

Conscious of the approaching, and lengthy, time of self-denial, people took advantage of their last opportunity to enjoy themselves. They did so by playing all kinds of games and watching various sports. Cockfights, wrestling and football matches were all popular, as was another unique form of entertainment that is now linked closely with the day — pancake races.

Because the coming fast would demand the total exclusion of eggs and fat from the daily diet, all the eggs and butter left in the pantry had to be used up. One of the favourite ways to do this was to make pancakes.

The pancake races, so legend tells, came about early in the

fifteenth century as the result of a housewife's absentmindedness. Just when she was frying her cakes the church bell started to ring, calling the people to the service. She dashed out of the house and ran to church, forgetting that she was still clutching her frypan. In fact, she continued to toss the cakes on the way.

The most famous of all pancake races is the one run at Olney in the English county of Buckinghamshire. It is supposed to date back to as early as 1450. Run just before noon over a distance of 400 yards (364 m), it was open to all housewives over the age of eighteen. They had to adhere to strict rules, even with regard to the way they were dressed. Their hair had to be covered by a hat or a scarf and they had to wear an apron, but never slacks. Contestants were also required to have lived in the area for a minimum of six months.

During the race, each housewife had to carry the still sizzling pancake in its pan and to toss it three times on the way: at the start of the 'sprint'; at an optional point on the route; and at the finish. The winner became the pancake champion for the year. She was awarded a Bible from the vicar and a kiss from the bellringer, who could keep all the cakes cooked by the 'racers'.

It is no wonder then, that Shrove Tuesday also became popularly known as Pancake Tuesday.

Carnival

*C*arnival, yet another name of this day, bids 'farewell' to the eating of 'meat'. Its Latin roots, *vale carnis,* say so literally, though the English word reverses the order. Originally, and more

prosaically, it refers to the actual 'removing' (*levare*) of all 'meat' (*carnis*) from the table.

In some parts of the world, particularly in the Rhineland of western Germany, it has developed into an occasion of organised merrymaking. Starting on the Thursday before Shrove Tuesday, it is celebrated over three days which, for good reason, have been called the 'three mad days'. People wear fancy dress or, at least, false noses. Masked balls are held and colourful processions, with superbly decorated floats and much pageantry, wind their way through the streets. Everyone is expected to let his or her hair down. Parodoxically, not to do so is regarded as foolish.

The meaning of carnival became so secularised that now, divorced from its religious origin and significance, the word is applied to many varied types of organised festivities.

Mardi Gras

Mardi Gras is the French version of the carnival and is yet another term for Shrove Tuesday. It means 'Fat Tuesday'. It is so called because of the French custom of parading a fat cow festively through the streets on this day. The fat animal was to serve as a live reminder of the lean time that was about to commence. Making up in advance for the deprivation to come, people used the occasion for unbounded revelry and frenzied frivolity.

From France the custom spread to New Orleans, then still a French possession. There it grew to such dimensions that the New Orleans Mardi Gras gained world renown.

Ash Wednesday

Ash Wednesday is the first day of Lent. It received its name from a custom that is still practised on this day, when the priest marks worshippers' foreheads with the sign of the cross — in ashes! It is a symbol of penitence as well as a reminder to the faithful, who show their grief for the pain Jesus suffered and for their sins, that 'thou art dust and unto dust shalt thou return'.

The ritual is all that remains of an earlier tradition in which ashes were emptied all over the heads of penitents, who used to present themselves to the priest clad in sackcloth. This followed the ancient mourning custom of expressing sorrow symbolically by putting on sackcloth and sprinkling ashes on one's head.

Purim:
The Feast of Lots

Jewish festivals are celebrated according to the lunar calendar and therefore fall on different dates of each solar year.

The Feast of Purim occurs either in February or March and is the most joyous of all Jewish holy days. It celebrates the Jews' deliverance from a fiendish plot. Its story, found in the biblical book of Esther, is read out during the services from a special scroll.

The name Purim means 'lots'. It refers to the lots cast, as in a game of dice, by Haman, a chief minister of the ancient Persian Empire, to choose the most propitious date on which to massacre all

Jewish citizens within the realm. His decision was the result of mere personal vanity. He had felt slighted because one Jew, Mordecai, had refused to pay him divine homage. Not revealing his true motive, Haman obtained the king's consent to exterminate the entire community.

His scheme was thwarted by the intervention of Queen Esther, a Jewess herself, who was able to convince the king of the selfish reasons behind Haman's evil design. A day of threatened doom was thus changed into an occasion of rejoicing.

The feast of Purim is celebrated by the distribution of gifts to the poor and to friends. Children particularly enjoy dramatising the ancient events and impersonating the biblical figures. At the services, during the reading of the scroll of Esther, they express their contempt for Haman by stamping their feet and sounding noisy rattles each time his name is mentioned.

Among the typical delicacies served on the festival are triangular pastries filled with poppy seed. Called in Yiddish *Haman-Taschen*, these 'pockets' are meant to recall the fiend's three-cornered hat. And Jews, usually not given to drink, may get intoxicated on this one occasion in the year.

Apart from all the jollity and exuberance, Purim is a day of thanksgiving and commemoration. It recognises God's providential protection of the Jewish people and the triumph of good over evil.

March

*M*arch, called after Mars, the Roman god of war, was originally the first month of the year. People have rightly wondered how any nation could begin the year by venerating a martial deity dedicated to death and destruction.

There were valid, but now forgotten, reasons. Initially, Mars was a Roman god of vegetation and fertility, and it was appropriate to worship him at the time of the renewal of nature. It would gain his goodwill and encourage him to fructify the soil and the cattle, thereby keeping away famine for the entire year. It was for this reason, primarily, that March was named in his honour.

For strategic reasons this god of fertility, endowed with life-giving power, later became a god of war, with all the slaughter it implied. Springtime was regarded as the most

suitable season in which to embark on campaigns. To ensure victory a god's help was needed — and that is how Mars' function was extended to the realm of war!

1 MARCH

St David's Day:

Wearing the Leek

The first of March is the anniversary of the death of St David, the patron saint of Wales, in about AD 588. On this day Welshmen all over the world honour his memory. Proudly, they wear leeks or, at times, daffodils. A wealth of traditions, based both on fact and fiction, embellish the story of his life and wondrous achievements.

Born of a noble family, David took up the priesthood. Soon he became renowned for his piety, missionary zeal and austere lifestyle. People came from far and wide to listen to his words and to ask for counsel and material help. Visiting many parts of Wales, he spread his message and established monasteries and churches at numerous places.

Legend tells that, whenever he preached, a snow-white dove sat on his shoulder. On one such occasion the crowd that had come to listen to him was so enormous that his voice could not be heard. Miraculously, the ground on which he stood rose ever higher, till eventually he was standing on top of a hill, where everyone could see and hear him!

David founded Menevia and became its first abbott-bishop. On his passing, it was called after him, St David's. Its cathedral treasures his bones, which were not discovered until 1866.

The association of the leek with the saint and its subsequent adoption as the Welsh national emblem has been variously explained. At the time the Saxons were fighting the Welsh. In one of the decisive encounters David advised his countrymen to wear leeks in their caps. Thus identified, they would be able to recognise each other, even in the heat of battle, and more easily pick out the enemy!

The Welsh achieved a resounding victory and were convinced that it was due in no small part to their following St David's suggestion. They therefore made the leek, which had ensured the survival of their nation, their cherished symbol.

Another tradition claims that the leek was a reminder of the saint's simple way of life. He had restricted his diet to water and wild leeks. No wonder that people referred to him as *Aquaticus*, the 'water drinker'.

The simple fact that daffodils bloom around the time of St David's Day may account for the wearing of this flower. Its choice may have been influenced as well by its being popularly known as a 'daffy'. Daffy, a shortened form of Dafydd, was St David's Welsh nickname.

15 MARCH

The Ides of March:

An Ominous Day

Ides, a pre-Latin, Etruscan word, means 'divided'. As in the ancient Roman calendar the months were divided into halves, the Ides of March referred to the fifteenth day of this month. It was the very day on which, in 44 BC, Julius Caesar was assassinated.

Caesar had ignored previous forebodings and warnings of threats to his life. According to the writings of Plutarch, he had also made light of an augur's admonition to be specially on his guard on the Ides of March. In fact, when on that day he was walking up the steps to the Senate house, Caesar encountered the seer, he almost tauntingly reminded him of his unfulfilled prediction. 'The Ides of March have come', he defiantly challenged. Ominously, the augur responded that though, indeed, they had come, 'they have not yet passed'.

Soon afterwards, on entering the Senate, Caesar was stabbed to death.

Through Shakespeare's play, the portentous association of the day was perpetuated and so popularised that, ever since, 'Beware the Ides of March' has been used worldwide as a warning of impending danger or calamity.

17 MARCH

St Patrick's Day:

'The Wearing of the Green'

Traditionally, 17 March is the date both of St Patrick's birth (in c. 385) and of his death (in c. 461). Though the patron saint of Ireland, he was not born on Irish soil. He was, most likely, of Scottish birth.

At the age of sixteen, he was captured by Gaelic raiders. Taking him to Ireland, they sold him there as a slave. Whilst working as a shepherd, Patrick began to ponder about God and came to feel his presence ever more strongly.

After six years, he escaped to the Continent where, possibly in Gaul, he studied religion. He then had a dream. It urged him to go back to Ireland to convert its pagan population to Christianity. He heeded the 'call' and in c. 435, this time as a bishop, he returned to embark on his mission.

His was not an easy task. The well-established Druids tried everything in their power to stop him. They even threatened his life, but they never succeeded in carrying out their threat.

Indomitable in his zeal, he managed to convert ever more pagans. He displayed his courage by challenging the High King of Tara. More than anything else, however, it was the miracles attributed to him that attracted the crowds.

The best known of these was his alleged banishment of all snakes from Irish soil. There are two versions of how he did this. It had become his habit on his visits to the various parts of the country to announce his presence by beating a huge brass drum. One day, he promised, he would use this drum to rid Ireland of all its venomous creatures. At the appointed time, he climbed Croagh Patrick, the mountain now called after him, which is situated just outside the present Westport in the county of Mayo. During his ascent, he beat his drum with such force that it burst! This made many in the crowd that was following him start to lose faith, especially when they saw a huge black snake suddenly appear. As it glided down the hillside its body was shaking with what the people interpreted as laughter. But suddenly an angel, sent from heaven, appeared and patched up Patrick's drum. When, with renewed vigour, he resumed beating it, the snakes began to vanish. Not one of them remained — or ever returned.

According to the second tradition, Patrick ascended the holy mountain ringing a handbell. On reaching the summit, he threw the bell over the precipice and, as it fell, hundreds of serpents cascaded into the depths with it! Time and again angels retrieved the bell, and Patrick repeated the wondrous act till no snake was left! Patrick's bell is now displayed in the National Museum in Dublin along with the shrine in which it had been kept reverently for centuries.

It is asserted that St Patrick's miraculous feat permanently endowed Irish soil and timber with a potent anti-venomous quality. The story goes that as King's College, Cambridge, was built of Irish wood, no spider ever comes near it. Irish soil was specially shipped to Sydney, Australia, to be deposited around the newly built Vaucluse House to protect its grounds against the intrusion of snakes!

When teaching the Irish the principles of the Christian faith, St Patrick experienced great difficulty in explaining to them the meaning of the Trinity. Ingeniously, he then used nature as an illustration. Picking a shamrock, the plant that grows in profusion in Irish fields, he pointed to one of its distinctive features: the way its triple leaf grew out of one stem. Had not God thus implanted the Trinity in the soil of their country? His message was well understood. The Irish not only adopted the dogma, but made the shamrock their own.

The shamrock's green colour, indeed, gave the Emerald Isle its special hue and name. The Irish wear the shamrock with pride, and particularly so on St Patrick's Day. The custom is known as 'the wearing of the green'.

* * * * *

St Patrick became one of the most beloved of saints, and every Irishman identifies himself by his nickname, 'Paddy'.

When he was about to die, the story goes, Patrick implored the people not to grieve overmuch for him. On the contrary, he urged them to celebrate his departure to celestial heights. As practical as in his use of the shamrock, he suggested that to alleviate their sorrow Irishmen should take a small drop of 'something'.

In lasting obedience and reverence, the Irish continue to observe St Patrick's Day in the manner ordained by their saint. They do the rounds and, in convivial gatherings, 'wet the shamrock'. Some authorities trace Irish men's love of their whiskey to this practice.

Patrick has been given credit as well for the making of poteen, the strong, home-brewed drink distilled from potatoes. Even the name poteen, it was said, did not derive, as is generally thought, from the 'little pot' in which it was made, but was a variation of St Patrick's name.

Many other customs commemorate the saint's birth and death. As, in the northern hemisphere, the date falls in March when the weather is often cold and windy, the celebration of St Patrick's Day includes the eating of hot Irish stew and the drinking of an abundance of Guinness beer, followed by strong Irish coffee.

Of the many parades held on St Patrick's Day in American cities, the largest and most renowned is the one in New York City, which proceeds along Fifth Avenue and passes St Patrick's Cathedral. Hundreds of thousands of people including numerous bands, join in it. Proud of the Irish ancestry of so many Americans, participants and onlookers alike display the shamrock.

The Paddy Waggon

St Patrick has travelled a long way and his influence can be found in the most unexpected places, even in the naming of the paddy waggon.

The majority of New York's policemen are of Irish descent. Early on, therefore, they were nicknamed 'Paddy'. It is no wonder that the vehicle they used for transporting people they had arrested to their precinct's station became known colloquially as 'the paddy waggon'.

Another explanation still maintains its Irish connection. Loving their drink, Irish Americans at times overindulged and, once intoxicated, became troublesome. Picked up in vans, they were taken to the nearest police lock-up, to be kept there till they had sobered up. And it was because of its numerous Irish 'passengers' that the vehicle was dubbed the paddy waggon.

'As Mad as a March Hare'

The month of March has one interesting, though rather confusing, association with the animal world. A well-known phrase describes some people as being 'as mad as a March hare'. The odd association has been given several interpretations.

Hares mated during this month and, while engaged in this pursuit, they appeared off balance. This interpretation, however, is probably the result of a misunderstanding. Initially, the month of March was not mentioned at all in connection with hares. The original expression spoke of someone being 'as mad as a *marsh* hare'.

Hares that lived in marshes had very little cover in which to hide when attacked. Their vain attempts to find shelter must have driven them to desperation and, as they ran frantically hither and thither, they appeared to have lost their minds. People therefore had every justification to speak of someone being 'as mad as [such] a marsh hare'.

April

*N*ature and romance have given us the month of April
and may have done so in one of two ways.

In the northern hemisphere it is the time when the
buds of flowers and trees begin to 'open up', to blossom.
Highlighting this delicate stage of natural growth, the month
was identified with it. April is derived from the
Latin aperio, meaning 'I open'.

On the other hand, recognising the significant part
played by the reproductive forces in this month, the Greeks
may have dedicated it to Aphrodite, their goddess of fertility,
beauty and life. April is, perhaps, merely a
shortened form of her name.

April Fools' Day

*O*n 1 April people play practical jokes on each other.

It all started long ago — with Noah, according to one tradition. Having spent months in the Ark, he anxiously waited for the Flood to subside. When he thought that at long last this had happened, he sent out a dove, hopeful that it might find some firm ground. He was mistaken. It was much too soon and the dove, 'having found no rest for the sole of her foot', returned to the Ark. It had been a fool's errand.

The date of the failed mission was said to have been 1 April which, because of Noah's folly, was called the 'Old Fool's Day'. Eventually, however, either the circumstances were forgotten or, more kindly, it was considered unfair that so decent, 'righteous and blameless' a man as Noah, should be remembered as the Old Fool. So the 'Old Fool's Day' was changed into 'All Fools' Day', which it has remained ever since.

Another explanation has much greater historical validity. It relates to the adoption of the modern calendar and the fact that, until the sixteenth century, New Year's Day was celebrated on 25 March. It frequently happened that this very day, so jolly and happy, fell during Passion Week, and sometimes even coincided with Good Friday itself. To avoid such an unfortunate circumstance, the authorities postponed the traditional New Year celebrations to 1 April.

Old habits die hard. When the calendar was reformed and New Year's Day was moved back to 1 January, some people did not keep up

with the times! They forgot all about the new New Year. Taking advantage of their confusion, jokers made fun of them. They paid them ceremonial (mock) visits and asked them for presents, making real fools of their hosts, who took them seriously.

It has also been suggested that the custom is a relic of the once prevalent practice of unlocking the gates of mental institutions and allowing the insane to roam at large on 1 April. Released from the asylum for this one day, they became the unfortunate victims of heartless pranksters who asked them to perform acts which obviously were beyond them. In every sense, they sent them on fools' errands.

Whatever the reason, 1 April has become a day licensed for mischief, though of an innocuous kind. It is a day reserved for laughter. But tradition also demands that all hoaxing must cease at noon. Anyone extending the time limit makes a fool of himself.

Palm Sunday

The Sunday before Easter is celebrated as Palm Sunday. It commemorates Jesus' entry into Jerusalem when the people 'took palm branches and went out to meet him'.

At the time, the city was thronged with pilgrims who had come for the Jewish Passover, which was about to begin. Many of the crowd, so the Gospels tell, greeted him jubilantly. They spread out garments before him and covered his path with branches they cut from the trees which, traditionally, were palms. They waved the fronds as symbols of peace.

This is the basis of Palm Sunday and the custom on that day of

bringing fronds to church to be blessed and carried in procession. Some of the fronds are kept to provide the ashes for Ash Wednesday of the following year. Others used to be taken home by the worshippers in the belief that they would act as a powerful charm against lightning and storms.

Maundy Thursday

Maundy Thursday is the day before Good Friday. Its name is derived from the 'mandate' (now rendered maundy) or commandment' Jesus then gave to his followers, to love one another.

That Thursday was the eve of the Jewish Passover and Jesus, joined by his twelve disciples, celebrated it by the traditional festive meal, remembered as his 'Last Supper'. Its symbolism survives both in the bread and wine of the Communion service and in the portrayal of Jesus as 'the lamb of God'.

At the meal Jesus and his twelve disciples made up a company of thirteen and people began to wonder whether this was the cause of his being crucified on the following day. The mere association of that number with his execution may have been largely responsible for thirteen's reputation as an unlucky number.

The Gospel report relates how at this supper, as an act of humility, Jesus washed his disciples' feet. This led to the custom — practised for many centuries — of those in high positions washing the feet of a selected number of aged and poor. In the case of the English monarch, their number corresponded with the years of his (or her) age. As well as washing their feet, the king or queen presented them with

much-needed gifts, such as clothing, food and money. Silver coins, specially minted for the occasion, became known as 'Maundy money'.

Good Friday

Good Friday is the anniversary of Christ's death. People have rightly asked how such a tragic day in the Christian calendar could come to be called *Good* Friday. Perhaps the name was adopted, because of its particular holiness, merely to distinguish it from all other Fridays.

There is, as well, a theological explanation of the name. According to Christian dogma, Jesus' crucifixion brought about salvation, as his death had atoned for man's 'original sin'. To emphasise the great good which had thus come out of evil, this day of gloom was designated — not so paradoxically after all — as Good Friday.

Another explanation that has been suggested is that the day's original name was 'God's Friday', and that 'Good Friday' is simply a corruption of this.

Hot Cross Buns

The custom of eating hot cross buns on Good Friday goes back to pre-Christian days and pagan worship. The word bun is derived from 'boun', the archaic description of a sacred ox. The ox was sacrificed at the time of the vernal equinox and a stylised

representation of its horns was stamped upon the festive cakes that were eaten on the occasion. Hot cross buns are also linked with early lunar worship. The round bun was the replica of the full moon and the indentations symbolised its four quarters.

Whenever the early Church realised that it was impossible to abolish ingrained ancient customs, it wisely adapted them to its own beliefs. Thus, it reinterpreted the horn marks on the buns as the sign of the cross, which was so appropriate for the day of Jesus' crucifixion. The symbol also proved to have practical value. It made it easy to divide the cake into four equal parts, which could then be shared by the worshippers when they broke their fast (the origin of 'breakfast') even before returning home after the early morning Mass.

Easter

Easter, which commemorates the resurrection of Christ, is the oldest and greatest feast of the Christian faith. Its name is derived from Eostre, the Anglo-Saxon goddess of spring, whose festival was celebrated at this time of the year.

The date varies from year to year because in AD 325 the Council of Nicaea decided that Easter was always to be observed on the Sunday following the first full moon after the vernal equinox. The date may fall any time between 21 March and 25 April. The Eastern Orthodox Church further stipulates that it must be held after the Jewish Passover.

The Easter Egg

The Easter egg is the emblem of renewed life after death, and of resurrection.

To all appearances an egg is lifeless, and yet out of it can come a new creature. Just as the chick is entombed, as it were, in the egg and brought to life in due course, so out of the grave the dead will rise to a new existence. That is why, from earliest times and in many cultures, the egg became a symbol of fertility and immortality.

The ancient Greeks and Romans buried eggs, or their replicas, with their dead and left baskets of eggs on their graves. Maoris used to put an egg in the hand of a deceased person before burial. As a gesture of consolation, eggs are traditionally served to Jewish mourners on their return from the funeral of a loved one.

In the northern hemisphere Easter coincides with spring, the season of the renewal of nature, when out of the dead earth new life is about to arise. It is a time of creation and recreation. Already, in pagan days, the egg represented this rebirth of nature at the time of the solar new year. The egg has a further, cosmic, significance, because its shape is seen as resembling that of the earth.

Christianity adopted the ancient symbolism of the egg and applied it to Christ's resurrection. Its display and use at Easter popularised and dramatised the joyousness of the event. The fact that all through the fast of Lent the eating of eggs was prohibited made them all the more welcome on Easter day!

Painted Eggs

*A*t first the eggs were dyed bright red — a joyful colour, and one appropriate to express excitement at the coming of spring. Red, as the colour of blood, also symbolised, and actually was thought magically to ensure, the renewed life-sap that was coursing through nature. To Christians, specifically, it was a reminder of the blood shed by Jesus for the good of man.

Various reasons have been given for the custom of painting Easter eggs in different colours. Christologically, it was linked with Simon of Cyrene, a Jerusalem egg merchant whom Jesus had passed on the way to his crucifixion. Out of his deep compassion, Simon not only accompanied Jesus but, leaving behind his baskets of eggs, helped Jesus carry the cross to the site of execution. On his return from Calvary he discovered that, miraculously, all the eggs were coloured! A Polish legend traces the practice of dying the eggs for Easter to Jesus' early childhood. To give her son some extra joy, Mary had painted hard-boiled eggs in a variety of colours — yellow, green and red. Other mothers soon followed her example. Only when the egg became the symbol of resurrection was the custom restricted to the season of Easter.

New Clothes for Easter

*T*o wear a new garment on Easter is an old-established tradition. It may well date back to the time when the year started in March and was celebrated by the wearing of a new garment. The

custom was even more appropriate for Easter, with its message of rebirth and regeneration.

The donning of a new dress on this festival recalls, as well, the former Easter (and Whitsun) practice of baptising new adherents and investing them with white robes for the occasion. Inspired by this example, and in memory of their own baptism, all the faithful then put on new clothes at Easter. (It was only natural and human for those wearing a new outfit to be eager to display it. This was the origin of the Easter bonnet and of the Easter parade, which are so popular in the United States.) Superstition reinforced the custom. People came to believe that, by sympathetic magic, a new garment would rejuvenate the wearer.

Those too miserly to acquire new clothes were looked down upon. Even the birds, once regarded as God's messengers, were said to despise them. To show their displeasure, the birds dropped excreta on the clothes of such parsimonious worshippers as they made their way home from the service. With the passing of time, people no longer remembered the exact circumstances. All they knew was that the bird droppings had 'some' meaning. Perplexed, and possibly influenced by wishful thinking, they interpreted such untoward incidents the opposite way — to be thus 'decorated' meant good luck!

The Easter Bunny

Bunnies jumping about are a vivid illustration of the joys of spring. Yet, originally, the Easter bunny was no bunny at all, but a hare. It was the animal sacred to the goddess Eostre. Born with

its round eyes open, the animal was chosen as representing the full moon, which was so closely linked with this goddess's feast.

As both rabbits and hares are prolific breeders, they symbolised fertility and abundance of life. No wonder, therefore, that both became associated with the festival that celebrated spring and the resurrection of Christ. The popularity of rabbits with children also helped to spread the tradition of the lucky Easter bunny.

How the bunny got its name is a 'tale of a tail'. 'Bun' originally was another word for a tail, and 'bunny' is its diminutive. A rabbit was so called because of its 'little tail'.

23 APRIL

St George's Day:
The Feast of England's Patron Saint

*H*ow St George killed the dragon to save the life of a beautiful girl is a well-known legend that has had a significant influence on historical events.

Although it all happened in Libya, it was far-off England that made the hero her patron saint. English warriors adopted St George's name as their rallying call, and the banner of St George used to be carried into battle before the kings of England.

Hardly any facts are known about St George. Even the dates of his birth and of his martyr's death (in c. 303) are the subject of conjecture.

A soldier in the Roman army, and a pagan, George abandoned his military career when, in the pursuit of his duties, he was ordered to

imprison converts to the Christian faith. He adopted Christianity and promised henceforth to dedicate his entire life to doing good and to spreading the Christian message wherever he went.

On his arrival in Silene, in Libya, he was told of a fearsome dragon that was terrorising the city by demanding a daily offering of two sheep. When the town ran out of animals the monster insisted on a human sacrifice in their stead. Sadly, the people submitted, choosing by lot the daily victim.

On the day of George's visit, the king's daughter had been picked. Trembling and sobbing, the beautiful girl awaited the gruesome fate of being devoured by the beast. George fearlessly confronted the dragon. He badly wounded it with his lance and then used the princess's belt to lead the now powerless creature into the city!

After returning the girl to her royal father, he killed the dragon. He explained to the king and the people that his Christian faith had given him the supernatural strength needed to achieve the feat. As a result, the entire population, of well over 15 000 people, converted to Christianity.

George then continued on his travels till he was beheaded at the order of the Roman emperor Diocletian, at Lydda in Palestine on 23 April. His martyrdom was in punishment for having reprimanded Diocletian for his cruel and inhumane acts.

The story of George's life and heroic deeds grew in the telling. People were convinced, moreover, that, as well as his fabled exploits, he had performed many other good works that were 'known only to God'.

English Crusaders first heard of St George, his feats and his fate while they were in the Holy Land. Greatly inspired, they carried his story home to England, where it was soon to capture the imagination

of their countrymen. The English came to feel St George's presence in their midst, so much so that eventually they made him their patron saint.

Mystery still surrounds the details of his adoption for this role. Officially, St George became England's patron saint during the reign of King Edward III when, in c. 1348, he founded the famous Most Noble Order of the Garter and placed it under the Saint's patronage. St George's badge — a red cross on white background — became the symbol of England. It was emblazoned on the standards of the army and on the English flag, and the date of his death was celebrated as St George's Day.

By a strange coincidence, Shakespeare, England's greatest dramatist, is believed to have been born (in 1564), and to have died (in 1616), on St George's Day.

25 APRIL

Anzac Day

*A*nzac Day is a national holiday in Australia. It is considered by many to commemorate the occasion on which Australia 'came of age' as a nation. Historically it recalls not a victory, but what ultimately amounted to a military defeat. On that day in 1915, the second year of World War I, the joint forces of the Australian and New Zealand Army Corps (known by their initials as ANZAC) landed at Gallipoli on the Turkish peninsula, at what is now called Anzac Cove.

Lacking support, outnumbered and with inadequate munitions, they were eventually forced to withdraw. In spite of this, many people

believe that their experiences and sacrifices gave Australians a sense of national identity. General Sir John Monash, reflecting on the campaign in later years, spoke of its far-reaching results. The evacuation had shown the true value of Australian character and discipline. If there had been one man on the peninsula who had disobeyed orders, the withdrawal would have become a disaster. It depended for its success upon the absolute and rigid obedience of every man.

Anzac Day is now a memorial to all those who have fought and fallen in every conflict in which Australians served. Solemn 'dawn services', held in all parts of the country, start the day, and these are followed by a march. The rest of the day is devoted to reunions of former service personnel.

30 APRIL

Walpurgisnight:
An Annual Witches' Convention

Walpurgisnight is a significant date in the occult calendar of the German people, but has attained world renown through Goethe's *Faust*. It falls on the eve of May Day, on 30 April. On that night, witches, warlocks and demons are believed to be abroad, riotously and lasciviously celebrating a tryst with the devil. Their 'convention' is held on some lofty summit, usually on the Brocken, the highest peak in the Harz Mountains. In actual fact, the occasion presents a combination of pagan and Christian traditions.

Originally, the festival paid homage to the god Wodan and the

goddess Freya who had given birth to Spring. To celebrate it, so it was credulously assumed, witches from far and wide joined in festive gatherings. They made their way there, riding through the air on broomsticks, pitchforks, goats and cats.

Women who attended those 'get-togethers' genuinely believed themselves to be witches. In preparation for the night they would rub their skin with a special ointment, which was made by mixing a variety of substances obtained mainly from poppies and deadly nightshade. Investigation has shown that the ointment had hallucinogenic qualities. It produced vivid, weird hallucinations in which the self-styled witches imagined themselves to fly up in the air and to engage in wild orgies with the devil.

Unaware that there was a scientific explanation, people believed in the myth. Terrified, they used every means at their disposal to counteract and nullify any possible evil effects of the witches' rendezvous. They lit bonfires, sprinkled herbs on the ground or nailed them to their barns. They made loud noises, notably by ringing the church bells, convinced that the devilish spirits could not tolerate the din and would turn tail! The Christian Church tried its very best to stop the ghostly 'goings-on' and to rid the people of their fears and superstitious rites. A strange coincidence came to their aid.

It so happened that the night of 30 April was also sacred to St Walpurga. An English nun, she had been sent as a missionary to Germany where, in AD 761, she became abbess of the monastery at Heidenheim in Franconia. Many miracles were attributed to her during her lifetime and even after her death. Oil that exuded from the rock of her tomb, it was said, possessed miraculous healing powers. No wonder that she was made a saint!

The Church, therefore, had no difficulty in appropriating the night of the devil and in dedicating it to St Walpurga. It explains why, with a slight change in the spelling of the abbess's name, it has become known as Walpurgisnight. It is still celebrated as such — now with innocuous rites, dances, songs and bonfires — particularly in the area around the Brocken.

Passover:
The Festival of Freedom

Passover is the 'festival of freedom'. It commemorates the Israelites' liberation from Egyptian bondage more than 3000 years ago.

The name Passover is derived from the biblical story which tells how on the night when a divine messenger slew the Egyptian firstborn (the last of the ten plagues), he spared, or 'passed over', the homes of the Israelites. Called *Pesach* in Hebrew, the name refers to the Paschal lamb, sacrificed as an offering of thanksgiving on the eve of the Exodus.

The Matzah

The festival, which also celebrates spring, lasts eight days (seven in Israel and in Progressive Judaism). During this time Jews abstain from any food that is leavened. The ordinary type of bread is replaced by unleavened bread', known as *Matzah*. Described as 'the

bread of affliction', it is a reminder of the suffering endured, not only by the Israelites of old, but by all people bereft of freedom.

The traditional explanation of its origin carries with it a special message — never to give up hope. Even in the most desperate situation, unexpected divine help might be imminent.

After centuries of slavery, many of the Israelites never expected to be free again. Redemption then came so suddenly, and the people's departure was so hurried, that they had no time to prepare ordinary bread by adding yeast to the dough and then waiting for it to rise. So the people simply mixed flour and water, creating flat, thin wafers!

The Seder Nights

The first two nights of Passover are known as *Seder* nights. The Hebrew word relates to the prescribed 'order' (or 'sequence') of the service followed. It is a home celebration in which the family reads the *Haggada,* so called in Hebrew because it contains the 'story' of the Israelites' exodus from Egypt. Editions of the *Haggada* are often beautifully illustrated.

Some of the Symbols

Numerous practices and symbolic dishes that are prepared on the Seder nights employ elements of sight, texture and taste to help people relive the events of the past.

Bitter herbs or horseradish (*Maror*) are a reminder of the bitter

times experienced by the Israelites during the years of their bondage —
and of the suffering of all who are still oppressed and deprived of their
freedom. ·

The colour and texture of a mixture prepared from grated apples,
nuts, cinnamon and wine known as *Charoset*, is meant to recall the
bricks the Israelite slaves were forced to make, even without straw to
bind the clay. Salt water is symbolic of the tears shed by Jews, and all
those who are persecuted, in their suffering. A roasted shankbone
recalls the Paschal lamb. A roasted egg (still in its shell) is reminiscent
of the festival offering once brought to the ancient Temple in
Jerusalem. Hard-boiled eggs served in a dish of salt water prior to the
actual festive meal reiterate and reinforce the theme of the entire
Seder service. The eggs symbolise, as they do in the Easter tradition,
how something that is apparently dead can become a source of new
life. It may well happen at a time when men are crying out in
desperation, as history has proved.

May

*M*ay honours Maia, an ancient Roman goddess of
spring. She was chosen to be remembered and
worshipped at this time of the year, as she was linked in
mythology with the growth of nature. The linguistic roots of her
name spoke of a mother, a nurse, and of universal increase.

An alternative explanation claims that political
reasons were responsible for the designation of the month. Its
name paid tribute to the Majores, who formed the
original Senate of Rome.

Israeli Independence Day

On 14 May 1948 Israel was proclaimed a nation. Its anniversary, Israeli Independence Day (*Yom ha-Atzma'ut*), is celebrated according to the Hebrew date, on the fifth of Iyar (which may occur in either April or May). However, should the day coincide with the Sabbath or its eve, it is observed on the preceding Thursday.

Prizes are awarded to those who during the past year have made the most valuable contribution in the fields of science, agriculture, literature and art. In a special ceremony twelve torches are lit. Originally each symbolised one of the twelve tribes of Israel. Now they represent the diverse groups, from all parts of the world, that make up the nation of Israel.

1 MAY

May Day

May Day — the first day of May — is principally celebrated nowadays as Labour Day, a holiday for the workers. Originally, however, it was a spring festival. It was observed to promote the fertility of all growing things on which man's life depended. Its ritual included magic and even the offering of human sacrifices. Bonfires, still lit in many places throughout Britain and Europe on May Day, are actually the remnants of 'bone fires' — part of those ancient murderous practices.

The floral decorations and dances that characterise May Day are

also relics of rituals that were performed, in order to force the pace of nature. The ancient Celts used to dance around a living tree in an attempt to arouse its spirit. Moreover, the maypole recalls primitive man's worship of the phallus as the source of reproduction.

Labour Day was proclaimed as late as 1889 at the International Workers' Congress which was organised by French socialists and was being held in Paris. It stipulated that the day should be set aside as a workers' festival in all countries. It became a worldwide tradition, marked by public meetings, parades and political speeches, and fostered primarily by trade unions and other representatives of working people.

Mother's Day

Thousands of years ago mothers were venerated as a source of new life by the worship of a mother goddess. A festival, dedicated to her, was held at the very time of year when nature renewed itself.

The Church later introduced Mothering Sunday, which was observed on the fourth Sunday in Lent. Apprentices living away from home were given a day's leave to return to their families. They brought a small gift for their mothers, usually a cake, baked either by themselves or their employers, and known as a 'mothering cake'. Mothering Sunday is still observed in Britain at this time of year.

The modern Mother's Day dates from early in this century. No other observance has spread faster from such small beginnings. It originated in 1907 in Grafton, a small town in the American state of

Virginia. Anna Jarvis, one of its residents and a spinster, was deeply devoted to her mother. She was upset at how much adult children appeared to neglect their mothers and was determined to change this attitude of indifference. After all, a mother's love was the only love that asked for no return.

One day every year, she felt, should be set aside to pay tribute to all mothers. To gain the public support necessary to make her wish come true, Anna started a campaign of letter-writing. She wrote to congressmen, labour leaders, doctors, mayors — to everybody who was somebody. As there was no one in the world who had never had a mother, she could appeal to everyone 'personally'. Hers became a true crusade.

On 10 May 1908, which was the second anniversary of her mother's death, she arranged for memorial church services to be held, both in Grafton and in Philadelphia, where she then lived. Thus she launched Mother's Day. The date, the second Sunday in May, has never been changed.

As white carnations had been her mother's favourite flowers, Miss Jarvis had them distributed at those very first services. She caught people's imagination and the letters she wrote hit home.

State governments took up her cause. The governor of West Virginia officially proclaimed Mother's Day in that state in 1910. Soon other states followed his example and, on 9 May 1914, President Woodrow Wilson declared the second Sunday in May as the official Mother's Day throughout the United States. It became the custom to wear white carnations in memory of mothers who had passed away and red carnations to pay tribute to mothers still living.

The celebration of Mother's Day was soon extended to include the giving of presents and the sending of greeting cards.

As so often happens in life, the very person who had inspired the idea was forgotten. While businesses made millions of dollars commercialising the day, Anna Jarvis became so poor that friends had to pay to have her cared for in a nursing home. She died in 1948 at the age of eighty-four. However, the day she created did not die with her, but lived on to be celebrated around the world.

Whitsun or Pentecost

The feast of Whitsun, celebrated on the seventh Sunday after Easter, commemorates the descent of the Holy Spirit on the Apostles, which is said to have occurred on this day. Because it was the 'fiftieth' day after the resurrection, it became also known as Pentecost — the Greek for 'fiftieth'.

The name Whitsun recalls a once conspicuous feature of the feast's ritual. According to tradition, the divine spirit which inspired Jesus' disciples at the first Pentecost enabled them to baptise an extraordinarily large number of people. In remembrance of this, the day was specially set aside for the baptism of converts who, for the occasion, wore white garments. These became so conspicuous a feature of the festival that Pentecost was eventually called after it and became known as White Sunday.

The tradition lapsed and was soon forgotten, but the name was retained. No longer understanding its significance, people contracted the two words into one, and *White Sun*day became Whitsun.

Shavuot, The Feast of Weeks:
The Jewish Celebration of Revelation

The Feast of Weeks — *Shavuot* in Hebrew — was so called because it followed seven 'weeks' after Passover. Celebrating the revelation on Mount Sinai, the giving of the Ten Commandments, Shavuot is the birthday of the Jewish religion.

On Shavuot, too, the Jew expresses thanks for the blessings of nature, this time for the beginning of the wheat harvest in the Holy Land. Synagogues are decorated with flowers and plants.

MONDAY BEFORE MAY 24

Victoria Day

Also known as the Queen's birthday or Empire Day, this Canadian holiday takes place on the Monday before May 24, which was Queen Victoria's birthday. Celebration of the Queen's birthday was a tradition during her long reign from 1837 to 1901, but it was only in 1896 that Clementina Fessenden of Ontario conceived the idea of a day set aside to honour Great Britain. The first Empire Day was celebrated in Canada West (Ontario) the following year, and after Victoria's death the two holidays were combined. Through legislation passed by the Canadian Parliament in 1952, Victoria Day became a statutory holiday.

Memorial Day — Decoration Day

The US Memorial Day, held on the last Monday in May, was first observed shortly after the Civil War. Its original purpose was to honour the war dead of both the South and the North, thereby healing the split and helping to make the nation one again.

From early times, it was the custom on this day to decorate the graves of the fallen with flowers. This explains why the day also became known as Decoration Day.

There are a variety of claims as to where, how and by whom Memorial Day was introduced. Traditionally, the credit is given to the village of Waterloo in the state of New York and to Henry C. Welles, a local pharmacist. In 1865 he is said to have conceived the idea and submitted it to a committee, which then organised the first celebration on 5 March of the following year.

The occasion was marked by the flying of flags at half-mast, a veterans' parade and processions to the three cemeteries of the village. Flowers were placed on the graves and the village was decorated with foliage intertwined with black ribbons.

As Americans subsequently had to fight in many other conflicts, the scope of Memorial Day was expanded to pay tribute to all American servicemen and women.

June

June pays homage to Juno, one of the great goddesses of ancient Rome. Worshipped as the Queen of heaven, she was also venerated as the guardian of womanhood and marriage, which explains why this month, placed under her protection, was favoured for the celebration of weddings.

As with the preceding month, June has been linked with Roman political life. One theory asserts that it was given the name to honour the junior branch of the Roman legislature, the Junioribus.

Derby Day

*D*erby Day, held annually on the first Saturday in June, is named after the five-minute race over one and a half miles (2.4 km) that is run on that day at Epsom Downs, Surrey, England. It has been described as 'the blue ribbon of the turf' and is regarded as the principal horse race of the year in all Britain, if not the world.

First run in 1780, the race was given its name, so the story goes, by mere chance. At a dinner party at his home, the twelfth Earl of Derby was discussing the inauguration of a race, which should be open to three-year-old horses of both sexes, with his friend Sir Charles Bunbury.

Both men had conceived the idea and, having resolved that the race should go ahead, were still wondering what to call it.

The obvious thing was to use one of their names. But whose? Neither wanted to give offence to the other, so they tossed a coin. Derby won the toss and the race has been called the Derby ever since!

SECOND SATURDAY IN JUNE

The Queen's Birthday

*T*he British sovereign has two birthdays every year — on the real date of his or her birth and on an officially proclaimed day. This explains why, although the present queen was born on 21 April, her birthday is celebrated on the second Saturday in June.

67

The day was not chosen because any particular monarch was actually born then. Indeed the choice had nothing to do with the needs or convenience of the monarch. Concern for the people's enjoyment was the major reason for fixing the date in June. Because the day fell during the summer season, it was most likely that the sky would be blue and the weather pleasant and therefore conducive to all types of outdoor events, games and sports.

Other considerations of a practical kind also supported the new date. Traditionally, the king or queen awards titles and decorations twice annually. Honours' lists are published both on New Year's Day and the monarch's birthday. To prevent the occasions from being too close together or, worse still, happening to fall during the same month, the middle of the year was chosen as the most feasible time to fix the monarch's official birthday.

'Trooping the Colour' forms the stirring climax of the celebrations. It attracts vast crowds. With the ever-increasing weekday traffic causing congestion in London streets, people experienced great difficulty in reaching the Horse Guards Parade off Whitehall, where the ceremony is held. To eliminate this problem it was decided to move the celebration to a weekend — a 'Saturday early in June'.

Trooping the Colour

Trooping the Colour has been described as 'the most impressive military parade in the world'. Ever since 1805, it has been part of the sovereign's birthday celebrations.

The custom, now merely ceremonial, originally played a most

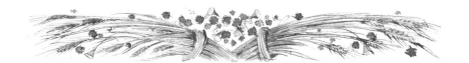

important military role. Until the Crimean War, to inspire troops to feats of bravery, an individual unit's flag was carried ahead of it into battle. Just as important was the flag's function as a rallying point if a company was in danger of being routed or scattered.

This made it essential for the soldiers to be totally familiar with their regimental colours and able to recognise them instantly, even in the heat of battle and the most desperate of situations. Any hesitation on their part could spell death for them or defeat for their company. For this purpose the flag (the 'colour') was paraded ('trooped') before the men daily. The custom was first practised in the seventeenth century, in the time of Charles II.

THIRD SUNDAY IN JUNE

Father's Day

Several people have claimed responsibility for the introduction of the modern Father's Day. Each of them, no doubt, thought of it independently, but the credit must go to Mrs John Bruce Dodd.

On the second Sunday in May of 1909 she was attending a Mother's Day service in Spokane, in the state of Washington. While listening to the sermon preached by the Reverend Dr Rasmus, dealing with the virtues of mothers, she wondered why no day of the year paid tribute to fathers.

Her thoughts were prompted by memories of her own father, William Jackson Smart. His wife had died young, and he had been left to raise six children single-handed. He had made every possible sacrifice for his family, doing so uncomplainingly. Mrs Dodd realised

that he was not the only such father.

After the service, she went up to the minister and told him of her thoughts. He agreed with her and, at his suggestion and with his help, she drafted a letter to the president of the Spokane Ministerial Association, setting out her proposal for a Father's Day. The Association, enthusiastically approving the idea, submitted it to the Spokane YMCA, feeling that its members were best suited to put it into action. Thus, in 1910, Spokane became the first city in the world to observe Father's Day.

Personal considerations on Mrs Dodd's part were responsible for the choice of the date. She wanted to perpetuate 5 June, which had been her father's birthday. But, as this was too close to Mother's Day (the second Sunday in May), she agreed to postpone its celebration by two weeks to the third Sunday in June. It was also at her suggestion that people, to show respect for fathers, began to wear a rose — red for living dads and white for those who had passed away.

In 1916 President Woodrow Wilson inaugurated the celebration of Father's Day in Spokane.

Nevertheless, the fight to gain official national recognition had not yet been won, and several further attempts failed. This led Senator Margaret Chase Smith, in February 1957, to accuse Congress of discriminating against fathers. 'Either we honour both our parents, mother and father', she said, 'or none.' It took another fifteen years until, in 1972, President Richard Nixon signed a Congressional Resolution, putting Father's Day on an equal footing with Mother's Day. At long last, Mrs Dodd had won the day.

In Australia, Father's Day is celebrated on the first Sunday in September.

July

*J*uly honours the memory of Julius Caesar and is the
first month in the year to be called after
an historical figure.

It was named after him at Mark Antony's
suggestion following, and in the same year as, Caesar's
assassination. Antony chose this month to pay tribute to
him as it was Caesar's birthday month.

Until the end of the eighteenth century July was
pronounced 'ju-lee', a pronunciation that was much more
reminiscent of Julius Caesar.

Canada Day

On 1 July 1867 the Dominion of Canada was born. On that day four separate British colonies with some three and a half million people joined in a confederation which was to grow into the great nation of Canada. The occasion was celebrated by the ringing of church bells, the playing of bands, the marching of soldiers and the lighting of bonfires in every township throughout the vast area that comprised Nova Scotia, New Brunswick and Lower and Upper Canada. The last two later became the provinces of Quebec and Ontario.

The historic moment was the result of a two-week conference held at Quebec. Seventy-two resolutions that were framed at that conference became the basis of the 'British North American Act' which was passed by the British Parliament. This made Canada a free and independent Dominion of the British Empire. At the time, Lord Carnarvon, the Colonial Secretary, who had moved the second reading of the Bill, stated: 'We are laying the foundation of a great state — perhaps one which at a future day may even overshadow this country'.

Scottish-born John Alexander Macdonald, who was to become Canada's first Prime Minister, was the leader of a Canadian delegation to London which was instrumental in securing the Act. At the meeting he had suggested 'The Kingdom of Canada' as the name of the new country. The British parliamentarians, however, rejected his idea. They feared that to refer to Canada as a 'kingdom' might offend the citizens of the neighbouring republic 'with whom the people of this [new] country would have to live in peace, if live at all'.

Tradition tells that Samuel Tilley of New Brunswick, another powerful advocate of confederation, had then proposed 'The Dominion of Canada' as an alternative name. He had taken the description from the Psalmist's passage: 'He shall have *dominion*…from sea to sea' (Psalm 72:8).

That is how the Dominion of Canada came into existence and why, for many years, Canada Day was celebrated as 'Dominion Day'.

4 JULY

American Independence Day

The fourth of July commemorates the birth of the nation. On this day in 1776, at the Continental Congress in Philadelphia, the thirteen American colonies adopted the document which declared their independence and separated them from Britain. In American tradition the date became so memorable that 'The Fourth of July' often takes precedence over its official name, 'Independence Day'.

The 'Declaration of Independence' proclaimed as self-evident truths that 'all men are created equal' and are endowed 'with certain inalienable rights', among which 'life, liberty and the pursuit of happiness' are paramount.

The observance of Independence Day became the most popular and patriotic celebration in the United States. Speeches, parades and fireworks are some of its traditional features. It is interesting to note that the word 'firework', previously referred to as 'rockets', was first used in connection with the day's celebration!

One of the many well-known figures called upon to deliver the

'Fourth of July Oration', was Daniel Webster, famous for his statesmanship and eloquence. The sentiments he expressed on the occasion are as applicable nowadays as in his time:

> *This anniversary animates and gladdens all American hearts. On other days of the year we may be party men, indulging in controversies more or less important to the public good. We may have likes and dislikes, and we may maintain our political differences…But today we are Americans all; and all, nothing but American.*

14 JULY

Bastille Day:

France's National Day

The French national holiday bears the name of a notorious Paris prison, the Bastille. Incarcerated in it were political prisoners who had fought for a more just society in which 'liberty, equality and fraternity' would prevail. Parisian citizens stormed this infamous gaol

on 14 July 1789, forcing the commandant to surrender. The event marked the beginning of the French Revolution whose impact was felt throughout the world. It is a proclaimed national holiday and is celebrated with fireworks, parades and dancing in the streets.

15 JULY

St Swithin's Day

The fifteenth of July is St Swithin's Day. It would have acquired no special significance were it not for a superstition attached to this day that persisted for a thousand years. It claimed that should it rain on 15 July, the rain would continue for another forty days.

Swithin was a ninth-century bishop of Winchester, England. A humble man, he left instructions that at his death his body should not be interred in the cathedral, as was a bishop's privilege, but should be buried among the poor in the north churchyard where 'the sweet rain of heaven' would fall upon his grave. His request was duly honoured, in 862.

Time passed and Swithin was raised to sainthood. The clergy now felt that the remains of so pious a man should not stay outside the sanctuary. Their rightful place was in a vault inside the cathedral. All the necessary arrangements were made to transfer his relics — on 15 July 971. But when, on that day, they were about to do so, it began to pour in such torrents that it was decided to postpone the project.

When, after forty days the rain had not abated, the people felt that this could not be a natural phenomenon. They interpreted it as a

message from St Swithin, protesting against the dishonouring of his wish. So the plan for removing his remains was abandoned and, almost instantly, the clouds dispersed and the sun shone again. Memory of this event survives in superstition; some country folk still look out every St Swithin's Day to see whether or not the sun is shining.

Subsequent research has disproved the superstition. In fact, on 15 July 971 St Swithin's remains came to rest inside the cathedral without the occurrence of any untoward incident. They did so, however, without being moved! As a result of an ambitious building program to enlarge the old Minster, the section of the old churchyard in which the saint was buried became part of a new 'shrine church'.

Records also indicate that it did not rain on that specific date, so that even this part of the tradition holds no water! Further investigations reveal not a single instance of continuous rain following St Swithin's Day. The maximum period of precipitation, which occurred in 1848, was still three days short of the traditional forty.

Tish'ah b'Av:
A Jewish Day of Mourning

Tish'ah b'Av is the Hebrew date (9 Av) and the name of the most mournful day of the Jewish year, falling in either July or August. A day of fast, it demands complete abstention from food and drink. The most ominous day in Jewish life, it is the anniversary of the destruction of both the first and the second Temples in Jerusalem (in 586 BC and AD 70). By an ominous coincidence, it was on this day in 1492 that the Jews were expelled from Spain. It was also the day in 1914 (1 August) on which World War I started.

78

August

August is named after Augustus, Julius Caesar's nephew and successor as ruler of Rome. He was originally called Octavian but, in acknowledgment of his distinguished services to the state, the Roman Senate conferred on him the honorific title 'Augustus' — 'The Majestic'. And it is this epithet by which he became known and is remembered. August merely omits its Latin ending.

The month was not chosen, as July was in Caesar's case, because it marked Augustus' birthday (which fell in September), but because the month had proved lucky for him politically.

The English August Bank Holiday

In the eighteenth and nineteenth centuries numerous public holidays — sometimes as many as thirty-three in a year — made the Bank of England close its doors, causing serious disruption to British commerce and industry. To make things worse, these holidays were not properly regulated but were frequently decided upon almost on the spur of the moment — to celebrate some special event, saint's day or anniversary.

There was a growing realisation that drastic rationalisation was essential for the benefit of the nation. The result was the introduction of the August Bank Holiday. It, along with six other annual official holidays, was to replace all other 'free days'. An Act of Parliament, referred to by its promoter's name as the Sir John Lubbock's Act, was passed in 1871 and decreed that on the first Monday in August all banks would be closed. Bills due on that day would be payable on the following day. Offices followed suit and the (so-called) 'Bank Holiday' developed into a people's holiday — with fairs, sporting events and other amusements.

The August Bank Holiday has now been moved from the first to the last Monday of the month.

September

Though September is the ninth month of the year, its name — from the Latin *septum* — refers to it as 'the seventh'.

The apparent miscount is not a mistake. It is the result of man's conservatism, his aversion to discard names, even when they no longer apply. September used to be the seventh month when, in the old calendar, the year started in March. No one cared to update the name when the calendar was reformed and the beginning of the year advanced by two months, to January.

Father's Day

(AUSTRALIA) See entry under Third Sunday in June

FIRST MONDAY IN SEPTEMBER

American Labor Day

Work ethics have always been a distinguishing feature of the American people. In keeping with this tradition the United States came to select a special day with the dignity of labour as its major theme. It was to be different and separate from the European May Day and to express the special contribution that hard work had made to the nation. It was, indeed, a public tribute to American workers. Labor Day was introduced by a law passed by Congress in 1894. It was proclaimed a public holiday, to be celebrated on the first Monday in September.

Its early champion was Peter J. McGuire, General Secretary of the United Brotherhood of Carpenters and Joiners of America. As early as 1882 he had drawn the attention of his countrymen to the fact that, though there were holidays of religious, civil and military significance, none was 'representative of the industrial spirit — the great vital force of every nation'. It was McGuire, indeed, who suggested the date. It had no historic meaning but 'would come at the most pleasant season of the year, nearly midway between the Fourth of July and Thanksgiving and would fill a wide gap in the chronology of legal holidays'.

Labor Day involves the entire American nation, and not exclusively the worker. Ultimately, it became a holiday for families. As it falls at the very end of summer, and just before the start of the new school year, families spend it on outings and picnics.

Rosh Hashanah:
The Jewish New Year

The Jewish New Year and the Day of Atonement are the two most important Jewish festivals, known as High Holy Days or 'Days of Awe'. Celebrated according to the lunar calendar, they might fall during September or October.

The New Year, *Rosh Hashanah* in Hebrew, is traditionally observed for two days. Far from being boisterous, its celebration is solemn and is distinguished by reflection, prayer and penitence. On Rosh Hashanah God is believed to examine the conduct of every person. Those who have gone astray are given an opportunity to recognise their failings, to amend their ways and to start afresh. Appropriately, the literal meaning of the Hebrew for 'repentance' is 'return'.

On this holy day of universal concern, the Jew asks God's forgiveness for all sinners and prays for the unification of mankind.

The Counting of the Years

Rosh Hashanah is also regarded as the anniversary of creation. Significantly, the Jew counts the years, not from any event in his history, but from the beginning of the world. While the actual number is certainly unscientific, it is highly symbolic. It is a reminder that people should view life not from a narrow, parochial point of view, but with a concern for the whole of humanity and the universe.

The Blowing of the Ram's Horn

The most conspicuous feature of the service is the blowing of the *Shofar*, a ram's horn. Its distinctive sounds are meant to rouse man's conscience and act as a clarion call for a renewal of faith and a return to God.

Eating Apples and Honey

It is customary to start the meal on New Year's eve by eating slices of apple dipped in honey. It expresses the hope that the new year may be rich in flavour and sweet and that everyone may, as the traditional Hebrew New Year's wish expresses it, be 'inscribed and sealed for a good year'.

Yom Kippur:
The Day of Atonement

The Day of Atonement is the climax of the 'ten days of penitence' with which the Jewish year commences. The most sacred day of all, it is a day for self-searching as well as the day of God's final judgment.

Like all Jewish holy days, Yom Kippur starts on its eve, at sunset. But it is the only time that the eve of a festival has been given a separate name. Known as Kol Nidrei, it is called after the prayer with which the service begins. Its haunting melody has made it world-renowned. For twenty-four hours, until the following nightfall, Jews fast, abstaining totally from food and drink. They spend the entire day in continuous worship in the synagogue.

Yom Kippur is called the Day of Atonement because of the reconciliation it is meant to achieve. The individual, estranged from God by sin and separated from his fellow men by his selfishness, is given the chance to become once again 'at one' with both his Maker and all other men. Truly, it is a day of at-one-ment. In the words of its liturgy it anticipates the time when 'violence [shall] be gone, when evil shall give way to goodness, when war shall be forgotten, hunger be no more and all at last shall live in freedom' — as 'a single family, doing Your will with a perfect heart'.

October

*O*cto, *the Latin for 'eight', gave October its name as,
in the old discarded calendar, it used to be the eighth
month of the year.*

The Oktoberfest:

A Beer Festival

A nineteenth-century medical opinion referred to beer brewers
and beer cellars as the best pharmacists and pharmacies in the
world. At one time religion not only supported, but greatly fostered the
drinking of beer. Monks largely contributed to the art of brewing.
After all, beer provided a nutritious supplement to man's diet during

the meagre days of Lent. Beer has always been a favourite of Munich citizens. They refer to it as their 'liquid bread'.

Of all the world's beer festivals, none equals Munich's Oktoberfest either in fame or in size. Once limited to only one day, it now extends over sixteen days. In spite of its name, the Oktoberfest begins in September and concludes on the first Sunday in October.

Its origin in the nineteenth century concerned not the drinking of beer, but the racing of horses. On 12 October 1810 a royal wedding took place between Crown Prince Ludwig and Princess Therese of Saxe-Hildburghausen. A spectacular horse race was a fitting way to mark the royal event. The race was run at the closing of the festivities and proved an outstanding success. Sixty horses from all over Bavaria competed.

The race became an annual event, drawing vast crowds of spectators. A biennial agricultural show served as an additional attraction. In 1818 the original one-day race meeting had developed into several days of exuberant celebrations, with thousands of people thronging the grounds. To cater for their needs and to quench their thirst, beer tents and booths were put up. No one then realised that this was the birth of the Oktoberfest, as it later became known. Now, in all the drinking, glamour and abandonment to enjoyment no one remembers the horses that started it all.

The festivities are officially opened when the Lord Mayor taps the first barrel of beer. A large parade of colourfully decorated brewers' drays and magnificent floats brings the festivities to an exciting climax on the first Sunday of October. Beer tents erected for the occasion provide an unending supply of drink and food and a carnival atmosphere permeates the entire festival.

Canadian Thanksgiving

Canadian Thanksgiving is very similar to its American counterpart, except that it is observed on the second Monday of October. It is traditionally a day of general thanks and, as in the United States, the main items on the dinner menu are turkey, cranberry sauce and pumpkin pie.

The first documented Thanksgiving day in Canada took place in 1763, when the citizens of Halifax, Nova Scotia, celebrated the Treaty of Paris, which gave Canada to Britain. In Ontario, Thanksgiving Day was first observed in June of 1816, to give thanks for the end of the war between Great Britain and Napoleon.

Through a parliamentary act proclaimed in 1879, Thanksgiving became an annual holiday for Canada. Between 1921 and 1931 Thanksgiving and Armistice Day were merged and the two were celebrated on the Monday in the week in which November 11 occurred. In 1931, however, Thanksgiving Day was once again proclaimed a separate holiday, and since 1957 it has taken place in October.

Columbus Day

Columbus Day — originally celebrated on 12 October — honours the discoverer of the New World, who on this day in 1492 set foot in the Bahamas. Its scope has been extended to honour

all the pioneers — European and African settlers — who have helped to make America great and strong. For this reason an alternative name now used for Columbus Day is Pioneers Day.

The official celebration of Columbus Day was introduced by President Benjamin Harrison on the occasion of the 400th anniversary of the landing. In a proclamation Harrison called on all the people to cease from their toil on this day — to express honour to the discoverer and to celebrate the great achievements that were subsequently attained. It was to be a day on which the youth, especially, should appreciate the patriotic duties of American citizenship and show 'gratitude to divine Providence...and for the divine care and guidance with which he directed our history and so abundantly blessed our people'.

24 OCTOBER

United Nations Day:

A Modern Anniversary

The formation of the United Nations was an attempt to achieve what the League of Nations had failed to do. In the words of its Charter, it was 'to save succeeding generations from the scourge of war...and to reaffirm faith in fundamental human rights, in the dignity and worth of the human person'.

Representatives of fifty-one nations signed the Charter in San Francisco in June 1945. It was officially adopted on 24 October and two years later this date was designated as United Nations Day.

Its purpose was to remind people everywhere of the necessity of establishing peace between all peoples, races and nations. It also sought to acquaint them with the aims of the Charter and the work done by the various special agencies that were created by the organisation: in combating disease and hunger, in giving relief in areas of disaster, in supervising the cessation of hostilities between warring factions, and in caring for those least able to care for themselves.

The emblem of the United Nations, emblazoned on its flag, is widely displayed on United Nations Day. Fittingly, it depicts a pair of olive branches encompassing the map of the world.

Hallowe'en:

A Chance to Scare

Hallowe'en is a contraction of Hallow-Even. Its name indicates its place in the calendar. Its celebration precedes All Hallows' Day, better known by its modern form of All Saints' Day. Literally, Hallowe'en is its eve.

Its origin goes back to pre-Christian days, to Druid beliefs and customs that were adopted by the Celts. For them the day was the 'summer's end' (*Samhain*) and the last day of the year.

As the power of the sun waned with the onset of winter, people were afraid that life, and not just the year, was coming to an end. They imagined that the night was haunted by ghosts and witches and, more particularly, by the spirits of the dead who were revisiting their earthly

homes. With the supernatural rampant, the night was full of danger and omens. Concerned with their survival, people employed every possible means both to fortify the flames of the dying sun and to chase away, or at least to pacify, the evil spirits. For this purpose they lit bonfires and, not infrequently, offered gruesome sacrifices.

Even after Christianity had succeeded in suppressing paganism, people continued to practise some of its customs. However, they reinterpreted them to give them new and innocuous meanings. Going almost to the other extreme, they transformed a fearsome night into an occasion of jollification, particularly for the young.

Most popular — and a typical example of the change brought about — is the game of 'trick or treat'. In early times, people in scary disguise went around on that night, asking for alms. For the gifts received, they would pray or fast for lost souls who, it was believed, would gratefully give their goodwill to the donors. People who did not respond to the request would be haunted by the spirits of the neglected dead.

Nowadays children don scary masks and dress up as ghouls and ghosts. They roam the streets, going from house to house, knocking on doors demanding a 'treat', usually in the form of sweets. They play pranks on those who do not comply!

As in earlier times, bonfires are lit, but now they brighten up happy gatherings. Pumpkin lanterns with grinning faces carved into them add a mischievous and bizarre aspect to the present-day celebration. While they make the night of Hallowe'en all the more eerie and spooky, they are totally divorced from the macabre roots of the festival.

Succot:

The Feast of Tabernacles

*S*uccot, a seven-day festival and 'season of gladness', starts on the fifth day after Yom Kippur. Its name means 'booths' or 'tabernacles'. It is derived from the *Succah,* one of the conspicuous features of its celebration, expressing the twofold character of the feast.

The Succah

A harvest thanksgiving, Succot recalls the gathering in of fruit and grapes at that season in the Holy Land and the shelters (*Succot*) the workers then put up in the fields and vineyards to protect themselves from the burning sun.

As a reminder of that joyous time and custom, Jews build 'booths' in the grounds of their synagogues. A small temporary hut, the *Succah* is decorated inside with flowers, foliage and fruit and roofed with branches. Pious Jewish families erect their own private *Succah* in the yard of their home. They eat and live in it, weather permitting, during the seven days of the feast.

The *Succah* also serves as an historical reminder. It recalls the forty years during which the Israelites wandered through the desert, on their way from Egypt to the Holy Land. Without a fixed abode, they had to live in flimsy, makeshift huts which they built wherever they halted. For this reason the *Succah* must be a simple, temporary structure.

Etrog and Lulav

*P*art of the prayer ritual on Succot is the symbolic use of a combination of plants and fruit referred to as 'the four species'. They comprise a citron, known as *Etrog*, and the *Lulav*, which consists of a palmtree shoot, some myrtle twigs and willow branches tied together.

Held ceremoniously aloft at certain parts of the service, they are waved in all directions, thereby proclaiming that God is everywhere. At the same time the diversity of the plants and fruit that make up the *Etrog* and *Lulav* expresses appreciation for the multiplicity of vegetation with which God has blessed the universe — for man to enjoy, and not to destroy.

Simchat Torah:

'The Rejoicing of the Law'

*I*mmediately after Succot follows a final festival, appropriately called the 'Feast of Conclusion'. It is a joyful conclusion to the extended season of holy days. It is traditionally a two-day festival which, however, Reform Jews combine into one. On its second day, separately called 'the Rejoicing of the Law' (*Simchat Torah*), the annual cycle of the reading from the *Torah* (the 'Law') is completed, and then recommenced. There must be no pausing in the learning of God's word.

November

*N*ovem, *the Latin for 'nine', has given November its name. In the old Roman calendar it was the 'ninth' month of the year.*

1 NOVEMBER

All Saints' Day

*A*ll Saints' Day, initially known in England as All Hallows' Day, commemorates, as its name says, all the saints, known or unknown. It was specially instituted to honour saints who had died without their sanctity being recognised.

Its celebration goes back to the seventh century when the Roman Pantheon, a pagan temple built to honour the 'All-holy Ones' (and

not, as is often assumed, 'all the gods'), was converted into a Christian sanctuary. On 13 May in about 610 Pope Boniface IV dedicated it as a church 'To the Blessed Virgin and all Martyrs'.

For more than a century an annual memorial service for 'All Saints' was held on the anniversary of this dedication. Pope Gregory III moved it to 1 November, on which day he consecrated a chapel in the Basilica of St Peter to 'All the Souls'.

Mere practical considerations, it was suggested, and not ecclesiastical or theological reasons, were responsible for the change of date. As the feast now fell after the harvest and no longer during the busy springtime, it was so much easier to look after the vast number of pilgrims who flocked to Rome for the occasion.

In the following century Pope Gregory IV (d. 844) decreed that All Saints' Day should be universally observed.

2 NOVEMBER

All Souls' Day

All Souls' Day, following so closely on All Saints' Day, was first celebrated in the ninth century. It was established out of solicitude for the souls of those who had died but were still lingering in purgatory, on their way to heaven. Prayers said on the day implored God to help them quickly to attain 'the fellowship of the heavenly citizens'.

Christians who rejected the belief in purgatory either ceased to observe All Souls' Day or, if they did so, extended their concern (and their prayers) to all the dead.

Guy Fawkes Day

uy Fawkes Day, celebrated on 5 November, commemorates the foiling of the political plot by Guy Fawkes and fellow conspirators to blow up the British Houses of Parliament on that day in 1605. They were Roman Catholics, and had been driven to such acts of desperation in retaliation for severe penal laws that affected members of their faith.

The incident has become known as the Gunpowder Plot because of the thirty-six barrels of gunpowder Guy Fawkes had concealed in the vaults of the House of Lords and which he intended to ignite whilst King James I was opening the new session of Parliament. With the government and all members of both Houses being present, the timing was perfect. Had the scheme succeeded, the entire leadership of the nation would have been eliminated in one blow.

Almost at the last moment, the conspiracy was discovered. One of the plotters was the brother-in-law of a peer of the realm who would certainly have attended the opening of Parliament. In order to save his life, the plotter sent him an anonymous message urging him to stay away. His suspicion roused, the peer informed the authorities, who instantly launched an investigation. This led to the discovery of the explosives and the apprehension of the conspirators. Guy Fawkes and his accomplices were arrested, tried and executed.

Though Guy Fawkes' name is the only one now remembered and 'celebrated', he did not mastermind the scheme. He was only the instrument chosen to execute it. As a trained soldier who was familiar

with explosives, he was the person best suited for the job which, as a fervent convert to Catholicism, he gladly accepted.

When the news of the plot and of the apprehension of the plotters became known, a wave of patriotism swept the nation. An Act of Parliament decreed that for all times 5 November should be celebrated by a thanksgiving service and as a public holiday. Guy Fawkes Day thus became an occasion of jollification, looked forward to particularly by children. Bonfires are lit all over Britain and fireworks are set off. But, most important of all, effigies of the wicked 'Guy' are burnt. For many days before the date, children go round collecting 'a penny for the Guy'. They used to accompany their request by this popular jingle:

> *Remember, remember, the fifth of November,*
> *Gunpowder, treason and plot.*
> *There seems no reason why gunpowder treason*
> *Should ever be forgot.*

In its own intriguing way the Gunpowder Plot has enriched the wealth of British ceremonial traditions. Every year before the opening of Parliament by the sovereign, Yeomen of the Guard, carrying lanterns, ceremoniously search its cellars for hidden explosives or conspirators. Following a prescribed route, they look into every nook and cranny.

Guy's name has become part of the English vocabulary. At first reserved for the effigy of Guy Fawkes, it was soon applied to any sort of 'guy', and has totally lost its contemptuous taint.

Melbourne Cup Day

Australians certainly love their leisure. They also worship sport. Though renowned for their egalitarianism, they are fond of 'the sport of kings'. And one race every year stops the entire nation from working. Even if they are not actually present — instead glued to their television screens or their transistors — Australians all over the country, of every age and from every walk of life, follow the horses running in the Melbourne Cup.

Melbourne Cup Day is fixed for the first Tuesday in November. The race is recognised as one of the world's greatest handicap races. It is held at Flemington, a Melbourne suburb which is called after a butcher who once lived there.

The first Cup was run in 1861. There were seventeen starters and, paradoxically, the prize — apart from the money (170 pounds) — was not a cup at all, but a hand-beaten gold watch. Archer, the winning horse, had walked to Melbourne from its stable in Nowra, New South Wales, a distance of 500 miles (800 km).

Remembrance Day and Veterans Day

At 11 a.m. on 11 November 1918 — 'the eleventh hour of the eleventh day of the eleventh month' — World War I came to an end and the armistice was signed. At first designated Armistice Day, this date was set aside to honour those who fell in this war. To include also those killed in subsequent wars, the name was changed to Remembrance Day in Britain and member countries of the British Commonwealth of Nations, and to Veterans Day in the United States.

A two-minute silence, starting at exactly 11 o'clock, movingly pays tribute to all the men and women who lost their lives during the hostilities. Poppies, chosen because of the poppies that grew among the trenches and graves on the battlefields of Flanders, are worn on this day in memory of the dead.

In Britain, Remembrance Sunday (the second Sunday in November) has now taken the place of the original date. At 11 o'clock sharp, silent homage is paid to the fallen, and a solemn ceremony is held at the Cenotaph in Whitehall, on which are inscribed three simple, but symbolic and meaningful, words: 'THE GLORIOUS DEAD'.

Veterans Day in the United States — as its name suggests — honours not only the war dead but all those who fought for their country in any war.

Thanksgiving Day

Thanksgiving Day is celebrated on the fourth Thursday in November and was instituted to express gratitude to God for his favours during the preceding year.

The day is highlighted by family reunions, traditional meals of turkey served with cranberry sauce and pumpkin pie, and grand 'processions', as they were initially called. A special spectacle and attraction is Macy's Thanksgiving Parade in New York City, with its giant floats and countless marching bands.

The earliest Thanksgiving was celebrated in mid-October 1621, ten months after the Pilgrim Fathers had landed in New England. They gathered to give thanks to God for their first harvest, after a most trying time of deprivation, 'general sickness' and numerous deaths. The surviving Pilgrims had every reason to feel relief and to rejoice when their efforts to grow their first Indian corn had proved successful.

The Pilgrims were joined by neighbouring friendly Indians, who soon outnumbered them, and what had been intended to be primarily a solemn and religious occasion grew into a joyous feast, with games, sporting events, the firing of guns and the sounding of bugles. And the planned one-day celebration extended to at least three days.

To start with, Thanksgiving Day was observed only intermittently. In 1863, however, President Lincoln in a 'Thanksgiving Day Proclamation' made it a regular annual national holiday. He invited all fellow citizens — 'in every part of the United

States and also those who are at sea and those who are sojourning in foreign lands' — to set it apart and to observe it 'as a day of thanksgiving and praise to our beneficent Father who dwelleth in the heavens'.

The Turkey

That the turkey became the 'thanksgiving bird' may be the result of mere chance. Four men, whom Governor Bradford had sent out to hunt game to supply the meat at the festive meal, returned with a large amount of wild fowl, many of which were turkeys. These proved so delicious that they set a precedent and have been retained ever since as the main course at the thanksgiving dinner.

The very name of the bird has its own fascinating story. After all, it seems odd, on a specifically American national day, to feast on a bird called after a foreign country. The apparent paradox is based on a misunderstanding and the turkey was really a most appropriate choice. In actual fact, it is an American bird and its name is the result of a curious error.

The Spaniards had brought the bird to Europe from Mexico, where it was already domesticated. It later reached Britain by way of Turkey, and this led the English to assume wrongly that Turkey was its actual home. And so they (mis)named the fowl after that country!

Certainly apocryphal is the claim that credits Luis de Torres with its naming. In 1492 he had accompanied Columbus, as an interpreter, on his first voyage of discovery, and was the first European to set foot on American soil. On catching sight of the unusual fowl, he was so

amazed by its size that, impulsively and at the top of his voice, he called out 'Tukki'! *Tukki* was Hebrew for 'a big bird'. Torres, a Jew by birth, had used it instinctively. His companions, unacquainted with the sacred tongue, assumed that he had identified the bird and adopted 'Tukki' as its proper name. However, mispronouncing the Hebrew, they called it 'turkey'. To serve cranberry sauce with the roasted fowl soon became another traditional feature of the thanksgiving dinner. It is probable that the Pilgrim women chose it not merely for culinary reasons but for its nutritional value. Lacking our knowledge of vitamins, they must have guessed intuitively the value of cranberries in the prevention of scurvy.

30 NOVEMBER

St Andrew's Day

On 30 November Scotsmen all over the world celebrate St Andrew's Day. According to tradition, it is the day on which, in AD 70, the saint suffered martyrdom. Lively parties, celebrated in typical Scottish fashion, honour his memory. The men wear kilts, haggis is eaten and plenty of drink enjoyed. Dancing reels and the stirring sounds of the bagpipes contribute further to the festive atmosphere.

Paradoxically, the saint so revered by the Scots had never been to Scotland. He never even knew of its existence! His only association with the country was the burial of his bones in Scottish soil.

Accounts of his life and death are indeed scant, though through

the centuries they have been embroidered by many a legend. A Galilean fisherman and early follower of Jesus, Andrew had been one of the twelve Apostles. After the crucifixion, he left the Holy Land to travel abroad and spread the Christian message wherever he went. It was a dangerous task, and one frowned upon by the Romans who were then ruling that part of the world and who regarded Andrew's activities as undermining the authority and divinity of their emperor.

They arrested Andrew two days after his arrival in Patras in the Peloponnese and, after flogging him, put him to death. He was crucified on the X-shaped cross now known by his name.

Its choice has been explained in diverse ways. Andrew himself had requested it, one version tells. He is said to have asked for a cross of diagonal beams because he considered himself unworthy to die on an upright one, as Christ had done. On the other hand, it has been suggested that it was the Romans who purposely and cruelly used this method of execution. It was bound to prolong his agony, and for this reason, too, they fixed him to the cross by cords instead of the usual nails. They had not reckoned on Andrew's extraordinary power of endurance, which enabled him to withstand even the worst of tortures. Indeed, he welcomed the extra time, which gave him the opportunity to go on preaching to the crowd that had gathered around him. He did so to the very last moment.

For almost 300 years the Saint's bones were kept in Patras. One night, in AD 368, the monk who was looking after his grave had a vision. An angel, appearing to him in a dream, told him to gather St Andrew's relics and take them by boat to an unknown destination. The monk did as instructed. After many weeks of sailing, he was shipwrecked at Fife, on the eastern coast of Scotland. He interpreted

this as an indication that God willed the saint's remains to be left there. He laid them to rest in a sanctuary he built for this purpose. It is the site of the present-day city and cathedral of St Andrew's.

The Scots, convinced that divine providence had brought St Andrew's bones to their country, made him their patron saint. They believed that he helped them in their battles and took good care of their country. As a Bible-loving people, they may have been influenced in their choice by the traditional representation of the Saint, in which he is shown holding a Bible in his right hand.

The Season of Advent

Advent is the season that extends over the four weeks before Christmas. Starting either on St Andrew's Day or the Sunday nearest to it — known as Advent Sunday — it ends on Christmas eve.

Its name, from the Latin *adventus*, points to the 'coming' of Christ — most obviously the occasion of his birth, remembered and celebrated on Christmas Day; but also his 'second coming' when, on the 'Last Day', he is expected to come and judge the world.

Once a solemn time, observed in penitence, Advent in some parts of the world has totally changed in character, particularly for the young. They look forward to the 'coming' of Christmas. Given colourfully illustrated Advent calendars, they eagerly count the days and the whole experience becomes for them a happy and exciting *advent*ure.

Fixing Advent wreaths outside the front door is yet another seasonal custom, expressive of joyful anticipation.

December

erived from decem, *the Latin for 'ten', the name December — referring to the last, and twelfth, month of the year, is as inappropriate in its modern context as are the names of the preceding three months.*

10 DECEMBER

The Nobel Prize Awards:

An Anniversary of Death as a Day of Celebration

he annual award of the Nobel Prizes takes place on 10 December. It is the day on which, in 1896, Alfred Nobel died in his villa at San Remo, Italy, at the age of sixty-three. The first distribution of awards did not take place till 1901.

Nobel's legacy amounted to nine million dollars. Invested in safe securities, the accruing interest was to provide money for awards 'to five persons, regardless of nationality, for valuable contributions to the welfare of humanity'.

The actual ceremonies for the presentation of the awards are subject to special provisions. Those winning the prizes in Physics, Chemistry, Medicine (which includes Physiology) and Literature are honoured at a brilliant ceremony in Stockholm. The Peace Prize is bestowed separately, in Oslo. There is a valid reason for this. Norway was respected throughout the world for its impartiality and no nation would doubt that the five representatives appointed by its parliament would make a fair and unbiased selection of the person who had done most in the service of peace during the preceding year. Each prize winner (both in Stockholm and Oslo) receives a gold medal, an illuminated diploma and an envelope containing a promissory note for the prize money.

Some extraordinary features distinguish Alfred Nobel's life, death and bequest. Nobel's invention of dynamite gave new impetus to the war industry and was responsible for the deaths of countless people. It has, therefore, been suggested that he established the peace award principally to salve his conscience and in expiation of the evil that his inventive genius had bequeathed to the world.

Paradoxically, Nobel himself had never thought much about the giving of any prize. In fact, he denigrated those he received himself. They had not been awarded to him, he maintained, for true merit, but merely because he had the right kind of connections with the people that mattered, or had entertained them lavishly.

A wealthy man, Nobel was determined that none of his family

should benefit from his fortune. This was not out of personal acrimony, but because of his conviction that unearned money never brought happiness: 'Inherited wealth is a misfortune which merely dulls man's faculties'. His family's loss became mankind's gain.

Nobel drew up his final will a mere two weeks before his death. He did so, not in a solicitor's office in a formal document, but on a torn half-sheet of paper at a coffee table in a Parisian cafe. No one else was aware of its contents until four days after his death! His own family had no knowledge that any will existed, and therefore no inkling of its provisions.

25 DECEMBER

Christmas

There are numerous Christmas customs, each with its own story and its fascinating origin and tradition.

Christ's Mass

Christmas is 'Christ's Mass', celebrated in honour of Jesus' birth. As no historic evidence exists to indicate when this occurred, festivals to honour the occasion used to be held at various times and seasons of the year until, in 350, Pope Julius I designated 25 December. He did so mainly to counteract the popular feast in honour of Saturn at the time of the winter solstice. This explains why many of the merrymaking customs of Christmas were adopted from the early pagan practices and then Christianised.

Xmas

The spelling of Christmas as 'Xmas' is not a modern abbreviation but a relic of ancient Greek. In the Greek language the letter 'X' — *shi* — looked like the 'X' of our alphabet. It was the initial of *Xristos*, the Greek word for Christ.

Early scribes were busy people and parchment, a forerunner of paper, was costly. To save time and money, they often shortened words, and that is how they came to use not the entire name of *Xristos*, but merely its initial letter. Even when practical considerations no longer applied, Xmas was retained, not only because it had become traditional, but because people believed, wrongly, that the 'X' represented St Andrew's cross. Perhaps an even more significant reason was that Christ's name was regarded as too sacred to be written in full.

The Christmas Card

he Christmas card was invented by Sir Henry Cole of London in 1843. The very first one displayed three illustrations. The central piece depicted a jolly party with plenty of food and drink. On its sides were representations of good works: the clothing of the naked on the left and the feeding of the hungry on the right. Below the pictures was the seasonal greeting, wishing 'a merry Christmas and a happy New Year to you'.

The Tree

he Christmas tree, with its green foliage and candles, goes back to ancient magical belief. Its evergreen was thought to ensure the return of vegetation and the victory of light over darkness.

Several legends exist about the first tree. When St Boniface arrived from England to convert the German pagans, he was determined to root out all that was heathen. Thus, in the city of Geismar, he cut down a sacred oak, which roused the anger of many of its worshippers. To pacify them, St Boniface planted a fir tree in its stead, proclaiming that henceforth this would be the symbol of their new faith. It so happened that the event took place on Christmas eve.

Martin Luther, the father of the German Reformation, has also been credited with the introduction of the Christmas tree. Returning home on a snowy Christmas eve, he lifted his eyes to the sky and was deeply moved by the beauty of the thousands of glittering stars which

seemed to be clinging to the branches of the lofty pines. Realising that words were inadequate to describe the inspiring spectacle to his wife and children, he had a sudden inspiration. Passing through the front garden, he cut down one of its small fir trees. This he put into the nursery and lit up its branches with many candles to create a beautiful representation of God's glory, just as it had appeared to him in the heavens on that cold winter night.

British royalty popularised the Christmas tree in English-speaking countries. Prince Albert, Queen Victoria's German-born husband, had a Christmas tree erected in Windsor Castle in nostalgic remembrance of his home. The royal example was soon copied, and the custom spread throughout the world.

The Candles on the Tree

The lighting of candles at Christmas goes back far beyond Luther's time and the origins of the Christmas tree. It was part of early pagan sun worship. Like bonfires, candles were lit in the depths of winter to strengthen the weakened sun, lest its flames die out altogether and leave the world doomed. When the Church could not abolish the ancient custom, it invested the lighting of candles with a new, and Christian, meaning. The candles were lit, so the Church taught, to remind the faithful of the first Christmas. They symbolised the divine light that then illumined the world. According to another Christian tradition, the candles were meant to recall the lights people lit in their windows at the time of Jesus' birth, to let Joseph and Mary know that they would be welcome in their homes.

The lighting of the candles has been associated, as well, with the period in Irish history when the Catholic religion was banned. Priests, living in hiding, nevertheless continued to serve the faithful whenever circumstances permitted. A Catholic family would spy out its chance. When it was safe for a priest to come into the home to celebrate a clandestine Mass, the family would convey the message by placing a lighted candle in one of the windows. In this way Christmas candles also paid silent tribute to people of all faiths who, in the face of persecution, remained loyal to their belief.

Tinsel

A legend explains why Christmas trees are decorated with tinsel. A poor widow was determined to give her large family a memorable Christmas, but all she possessed was a tree. After spending many hours trimming it, she fell asleep, exhausted. Soon afterwards, spiders visited her home. They wove their webs all over the branches of the tree — and created the original tinsel!

To reward the widow's goodness, the Christ child is said to have miraculously changed the spider webs into silver threads which, reflecting light in magic brilliance, outshone anything ever seen before.

Yuletide and the Yule Log

Yuletide, as an alternative name for the season of Christmas, goes back to a pre-Christian feast — the Scandinavian celebration of Juul, observed at the same time of the year. Its name, referring to a 'wheel', represented the annual revolution of the sun which then was at its very lowest. Originally, the yule log was lit as a magical source of much-needed fuel for the heavenly body. It subsequently became symbolic of the light, warmth and life-giving power of the returning sun.

Christianity adopted the log and it became the custom on Christmas eve to place it on the hearth. It was kept burning for at least twelve hours, its glow adding extra warmth and enhancing the atmosphere of the festival.

Strict rules had to be followed in everything pertaining to the log. It could never be purchased. It could be received as a gift, be part of a tree grown on one's own property or just be picked up. It had to be kindled with a fragment of the previous year's log which had been specially preserved for this purpose, and its fire was never to be permitted to go out by itself.

Holly

Holly, an evergreen, symbolises deathlessness. The shrub's most conspicuous features have been associated with Jesus. Its bright red berries were seen as the drops of blood he shed on the cross,

their colour also representing the burning love for God in the hearts of the faithful. The plant's prickly leaves recollect the crown of thorns the Roman soldiers placed on Jesus' head when mocking him as 'the king of the Jews'.

Santa Claus

The original Santa Claus was St Nicholas, a fourth-century bishop of Myra in Asia Minor, now part of Turkey. 'Santa Claus' is merely an adaptation of Sinter Klaas, the Dutch rendering of his name.

All that is known of him is that he was a man of great piety and compassion who had to suffer much persecution. Soon after his death, however, he became the subject of numerous legends and was made the patron saint of a great number of places and people.

One of the stories related how he restored life to three schoolboys. They had been murdered and their bodies dismembered. His miraculous deed made him the favourite of children, who came to love him as Santa Claus.

The Christmas Stocking

St Nicholas, so yet another story goes, was also deeply concerned about three lovely sisters, living on the outskirts of a city. Desperately poor and destitute, they were tempted to sell their bodies.

Nicholas was determined to save the girls from prostitution. One

night he went to their home and, unnoticed, dropped three pieces of gold into it through the smoke-hole (chimneys did not yet exist at the time). The coins did not fall on to the hearth as he had expected, but into the sisters' stockings, which they had hung up near the fire to dry. Nothing could describe their happiness when, next morning, they found the fortune. Ever since, people — unaware of the legendary origins of the custom — hang up stockings, hoping to receive similarly pleasant surprises and gifts.

Where Did Santa Get His Sleigh and Reindeer?

A father's wish to give his children a memorable Christmas created the popular figure of Santa, depicted as arriving in a sleigh pulled by eight reindeer.

The father was Dr Clement Clarke Moore, Professor of Oriental and Greek Literature at the New York General Theological Seminary and the author of many scholarly works. On a cold winter's night in 1822, two days before Christmas, he sat down with his two little daughters in front of a blazing fire in their New York home to read them a poem he had specially written for them for Christmas. He had called it 'A Visit from St Nicholas'. It portrayed Santa 'dressed all in furs from his head to his foot' with 'a bundle of toys flung on his back'. He had a broad face and a round belly 'that shook when he laughed like a bowl full of jelly'. Moore pictured him as chubby and

plump, travelling in his sleigh pulled by reindeer! The words imaginatively recall his vision:

> *...when what to my wondering eyes should appear*
> *But a miniature sleigh and tiny reindeer...*
> *More rapid than eagles*
> *His coursers they came*
> *And he whistled and shouted and called them by name*
> *'Now Dasher! Now Dancer!*
> *Now Prancer! And Vixen!*
> *On Comet! On Cupid!*
> *On Donner and Blitzen!...*
> *Now dash away! Dash away! Dash away all!'*

This is how Santa's sleigh and reindeer first entered the folklore of Christmas.

Dr Moore had never intended to publish his poem. A friend of the family, very much taken by it, asked for a copy. The following year she sent it, anonymously and without informing Dr Moore, to a journal in Troy in the state of New York. The journal published it in a Christmas edition.

Other papers reprinted the poem, making it ever more popular. None, however, gave credit to its author. Dr Moore himself possibly felt that, as a professor of considerable standing, he should not admit that he had written it. Only in 1844 — twenty-two years after he had first read it out to his children — did he acknowledge his authorship. He then included 'A Visit from St Nicholas' in a collection of his poetry.

Meanwhile, his figure of Santa travelling in a reindeer-pulled sleigh had caught the people's imagination. It became so popular that it was taken for granted.

It is ironic that, except for a few experts, no one knows anything of the erudite work of the learned professor. His sole but enduring legacy is the image of Santa he presented to the world in a jingle he originally never intended to see published!

Father Christmas

The pot-bellied, bearded and bell-ringing Father Christmas is of even more recent origin. He was created by Thomas Nast, an American cartoonist, in drawings he made for *Harper's Weekly* over a period of twenty years from 1863. He based them on Clement Clarke Moore's poem. His series of illustrations gradually developed from the professor's fat, small, elf-like creature into the Father Christmas now known to all.

Rudolph the Red-nosed Reindeer

Every Christmas season the Chicago-based mail order store of Montgomery Ward used to distribute as a free gift (and advertisement) a colouring book for children. Until 1939 the firm obtained copies of these booklets from a local manufacturer. In that year, however, the management felt that Montgomery Ward had all the facilities needed to produce them on its own premises. This would not

only save the firm lots of expense but would allow it to present the booklet in a totally novel form.

Robert (Bob) May, a 35-year-old employee working in the copy department, was given the task. It was suggested that he should create some new, lovable, creature, similar to the popular 'Ferdinand, the Bull'.

Unfortunately, the job came at the worst possible time for him. He was deeply worried as his wife was terminally ill and the medical bills had put him greatly into debt. Despite his anguish he accepted the job. He decided that his booklet should give a message of hope to the many people who, like him, were facing desperate problems.

That is how he came to create the reindeer that he called Rudolph, which was to pull Santa Claus's sleigh. A shiny red nose would make other animals laugh at and make fun of Rudolph. But this very defect was to prove an advantage. Like the strong headlight of a car, the shiny nose would penetrate the densest fog, guiding Santa to bring hope, comfort and happiness to those who lived far away, in dark, isolated and lonely regions.

At first, his boss rejected the idea. May persisted. Remembering the Chinese saying that a picture was more powerful than a thousand words, he asked Denver Gillen, a friend in the art department, to draw the reindeer of his imagination. He then resubmitted Rudolph with the red nose, and this time his boss was enchanted.

When, on the following Christmas, his booklet appeared, it immediately caught people's imagination. Children lapped up the story of Rudolph, and the first print of 3 million copies had to be followed

instantly by many more. In 1949 Johnny Marks wrote the song 'Rudolph the Red-nosed Reindeer' which, with its catchy tune and a first rendition by Gene Autry, was to conquer the world.

Gifts

The giving of Christmas presents can be traced to an ancient Roman custom practised at that time of the year. When the pagan tradition was Christianised, it was said to relate to the gifts of gold, frankincense and myrrh the Magi had carried with them when they had come from the East to pay homage to the newborn Christ child.

'Silent Night, Holy Night'

When, on Christmas eve of 1818 in the Austrian village of Oberndorf, Father Josef Mohr was preparing his church for midnight Mass, he was most upset to discover that the organ did not play. Mice had eaten away part of its bellows!

As it was too late to have the damage repaired, he thought of an alternative way of giving the service solemnity and beauty. He asked Franz Gruber — the local schoolmaster who was also an amateur composer and, like Mohr, played the guitar — to set to music a poem he had written on the theme of Christmas. But it had to be ready that same night.

That is how 'Silent Night, Holy Night' was sung for the first time — as a duet, sung and accompanied on two guitars by the priest and the teacher in that village church. It all came about because of the proverbial church mice!

News travelled fast, and the hymn's beauty and the circumstances of its creation made it popular far and wide. Almost a hundred years later, Bing Crosby's rendition made it even more famous.

The Singing of Carols

Traditionally, the singing of carols at Christmas time commemorates the song the angels sang when they appeared to the shepherds at Bethlehem to announce Jesus' birth.

The present-day meaning of carol is far removed from its original one. A carol was once a secular dance which was performed at any time of the year. Holding hands, people formed a ring and as they circled around they joined in song. Because the configuration of the participants in this 'ring-dance' reminded onlookers of a coronet — *corolla* in Latin — they called it a 'carol'. The name was later transferred from the dance to the song itself.

By the sixteenth century carols had become a particularly popular feature of the Christmas season and were eventually reserved for it alone. The subject of the songs also came to relate exclusively to Christmas.

Another development followed. For some time Christmas carols were sung only in church, and only by the bishop and the clergy. But this situation did not last for long. The carols caught the people's imagination and were soon sung in the streets and in public places, in joyful celebration of the birth of Christ. Many of them dealt with the theme of Christmas in the most varied and imaginative ways.

Noel

*N*oël, the French word for Christmas, is derived from the Latin (*dies*) *natalis,* meaning 'birthday'. It became established in English through the popular carol.

The word Noel has become the subject of fanciful folk etymology, in which meanings that go far beyond the Latin root have been ascribed to it. Noel was traced to *nouvelles,* the French for the (good) 'news', because this is what the birth of Christ had brought to the

world. Others recognised in Noel a corrupted rendering of the joyful claim that, with the saviour's coming, everything was 'now well'. A third interpretation suggests that Christmas was called Noel because for those who accepted Jesus as Messiah there would be 'no hell'.

Kissing under the Mistletoe

Kissing under the mistletoe, now a romantic and innocent practice, originated in the early belief that this plant, which was green even in winter, could produce and promote sexual power. It was regarded as so potent that in some parts of the world mistletoe was used magically to increase the productivity of the soil, as a fertility 'drug' for cattle, and as a cure for sterility in humans.

The Druids worshipped the mistletoe. A parasitic plant, it grew intertwined with the branches of oak trees, which were also objects of veneration for the Druids. Clad in white robes, Druid priests used to cut the 'golden bough' of the mistletoe with golden sickles and then distribute bunches of the plant to the faithful.

Although the mistletoe's fabled aphrodisiac role is now long forgotten, a vestige of it is retained in the romantic Christmas custom with which the plant is associated.

Boxing Day

*T*he day after Christmas is St Stephen's Day, named in honour of Christianity's first martyr. In Britain and Commonwealth countries, however, it is known as Boxing Day. The name has nothing to do with the prize fights or the sport of pugilism, but refers to a simple box. Furthermore, what really mattered was not the box itself, but what it contained — a gift (in kind or cash) that was handed to people such as postmen and tradesmen on this day, in recognition of 'services rendered' throughout the year.

It all started, like so many of our traditions, in ancient Rome where, at the time of the Saturnalia, people exchanged presents. The Church tried to discourage the custom but, failing to do so, gave it instead a new and religious meaning. Any material gift received had to be used for the spiritual benefit of the donor, to pay for special prayers or Masses offered on his behalf.

Before a ship left port, for instance, a priest put a box on board, dedicated to the saint under whose protection she sailed. As a penance for their misdemeanours, seamen were expected to make individual contributions to the box, which was opened only on the ship's homecoming. In return for the money collected the priest then said Mass for the men, entreating forgiveness for offences they had committed during the voyage. It was an early kind of *Christ's Mass*, and the box into which the offerings had been placed became known as the *Christ's Mass Box*. The money itself was distributed among the poor.

The box became the symbol of church charity and was given a permanent place in every church sanctuary. Traditionally it was opened immediately after the morning service on Christmas Day. The parish priest doled out the money it contained to the needy on the following day which, for this reason, became known as *Box*ing Day. For very good reason most of the boxes were made not of wood, but of earthenware. To open them, one had to break them.

Eventually, the religious custom once again became secularised and on the day after Christmas apprentices, carrying boxes, called on their master's clients to collect tips.

The use of boxes has been discarded, but the gifts are expected just as before, and not only by apprentices. Oddly enough, the gratuity is still referred to as a 'Christmas box'.

Chanukah:

The Feast of Lights

*C*hanukah, the Feast of Lights, usually falls some time in December. It lasts eight days. Though regarded a 'minor' festival, on which Jews are permitted to carry out their normal daily work, its message is major and universal. It speaks of the supremacy of spiritual values over material forces and commemorates the survival of monotheism when a despotic pagan empire tried to destroy it.

Chanukah means 'consecration'. The feast celebrates the rededication (in 165 BC) by the Maccabees of the Temple in Jerusalem after it had been desecrated by three years of pagan worship. Its story is told in the Book of the Maccabees in the Apocrypha.

Though greatly outnumbered, the small band of Maccabees were able, by the strength of their faith, to oust the invader who had tried to force his pagan philosophy and way of life on all the countries he conquered.

The Menorah and the Lighting of the Candles

*N*ightly during this festival, Jews light the *Menorah*, an eight-branched candelabrum. They do so in their synagogues and in their homes. On the first evening a single candle is lit and the number is increased by one on each evening until, on the last night, all lights shine forth.

The candelabrum is named and fashioned after the original Menorah, a seven-branched candlestick that once stood in the Temple and has become the symbol of the Jewish faith.

A legend explains the practice of lighting it on eight consecutive nights. When, at long last, the Maccabees had expelled the invader and cleansed the Temple, they were about to rekindle its perpetual lamp, which was the symbol of God's continuous care and which had been extinguished by the foe. But all they could find was a single jar of undefiled oil, sufficient to last only one day. Miraculously, it burnt for a full eight days, the time it took to prepare new oil for the sacred lamp.

Each of the eight nights offers its own excitement. Children receive gifts. Potato pancakes, known as 'Latkes', specially prepared for

the occasion, are shared by the family, who also join in an innocent gamble with 'Dreidels'. These are small spinning tops, marked on each of their four sides with a Hebrew letter which indicates how much the player has won or lost.

But the big event is the kindling of the Menorah and the joint chanting of the Chanukah hymn, which praises God as the 'Rock of Ages'. The candelabrum is then placed near a window to 'publicise the miracle' and as a symbol of the light of freedom that must shine for all races and peoples of the world.

Chanukah, indeed, is a happy festival, looked forward to each year by young and old.

31 DECEMBER

New Year's Eve

An atmosphere of hilarity distinguishes the New Year's eve celebrations. Farewelling the old year, people welcome the new year boisterously, feasting and drinking until the revelries reach their climax at the stroke of midnight.

What is no longer understood is that all the fun and noise originated in fear. People believed that on the night of the last day of the year all evil spirits were let loose and devilish forces were all around. From very early times, then, they used every possible means to drive the evil spirits away, so that they could start the New Year unharmed and unimpeded.

Those evil spirits, as the servants of the forces of darkness, were, it was thought, afraid of light. To scare them away, people set off

fireworks. The demons were thought to be equally averse to noise. It made them turn tail! At midnight, then, the most critical moment of all, people combined to produce a deafening racket.

The practice survives in the present New Year custom of ringing church bells, blowing horns, sounding sirens and exploding fire crackers on the stroke of midnight.

The New Year's eve celebrations thus started as an anti-demonic ritual, designed to ensure that the beginning of the New Year would be totally free from evil. The way the year started magically determined the rest of its course.

31 DECEMBER

Hogmanay

To Scots all over the world 31 December is known as Hogmanay. Several explanations have been given as to the meaning and origin of the name.

The name has been said to derive from *aguillaneuf*, the Old French (Norman) word for the last day of the year. The Scots merely adopted it and then adapted it to their tongue.

Others have claimed that the word is a contraction of a French wish for '[good luck] to the mistletoe of the New Year' — *au-gui-l'an-neuf*. After all, the mistletoe, once the sacred plant of the Druids, played a prominent role at Christmas time, and the Scots may well have taken it over for their celebration of Hogmanay. Yet another explanation sees in the obscure word, a corruption of the Old French *au gui menez*, 'lead on to the mistletoe'.

Hogmanay also is said to have been an ancient Scottish exclamation, uttered when asking for or presenting a gift. This would link the name with a custom once associated with the day. Groups of youngsters, carrying sacks, went from door to door soliciting gifts — usually oatmeal cakes. They continued their visits till the sacks were full, then feasted on what they had collected. The children invoked God's blessing on all who welcomed them, and they marked the households of those who let them go empty-handed, mainly by erecting in front of them small cairns, which proclaimed the owner's miserliness to every passer-by. The custom survives in the 'trick or treat' of the American Hallowe'en.

A specifically Christian explanation suggests that the name of Hogmanay developed from the French *Homme est né* — 'Man is born'.

The celebration of Hogmanay is distinguished most of all by its characteristic Scottish features. These include the playing of bagpipes, the drinking of whisky and punch and the enjoyment of favourite Scottish dishes.

31 DECEMBER
'Auld Lang Syne'

At the very end of the old year people gather to celebrate the occasion and join in singing 'Auld Lang Syne'. They do so standing up, crossing their arms in front of them and simultaneously clasping the hands of their neighbours on either side. Rhythmically they swing their arms in time with the nostalgic, sentimental song.

Robert Burns, who is usually credited with the words, admitted that he was not their author, but that he had first heard them sung by an old man. Deeply moved, he had adopted them for the poem he wrote in 1788. He not only entitled it 'Auld Lang Syne' (meaning literally 'old long since' but more freely translated as 'the good old days') but he ended each verse with these words.

The melody of the song is not his either. In a letter Burns once explained that 'untill I am compleat master of a tune, in my own singing (such as it is) I never can compose for it'. The melody is attributed to William Shield, a well-known composer at the time, who based it on a folk tune. Part of the overture to his opera *Rosina*, it was first performed in 1783 in London's Covent Garden. Shield specially stipulated that the orchestra should play it in a manner that simulated the sound of Scottish bagpipes.

The air, the words and the ritual all combine to make 'Auld Lang Syne' a fitting and moving conclusion to the year.

Muslim Holy Days

*T*he year of Islam follows the lunar calendar. This makes it eleven days shorter than the solar year as represented by the Gregorian calendar. As a result, its festivals and celebrations may fall at any season. They always commence at sunset.

Ramadan:
A Month of Fasting

*R*amadan, the ninth month of the Muslim year, is unique in the history of religion. It is one of the most sacred months in Islam because during this month the Quran was revealed to Muhammed. For the entire month it is compulsory for Muslims to fast from dawn to sunset. During the hours of daylight they must not eat, drink, smoke or have sexual intercourse. Children under the age of twelve, though not expected to keep the entire fast, are trained to eat less and are encouraged to fast on at least some of the days. Anyone too old, weak or sick to observe the fast is exempt, but is expected, means permitting, to compensate by providing food for the poor.

The reasons for the fast are manifold. It gives the faithful a proper sense of proportion and values and makes them realise that there are more significant things in life than eating, drinking and sex. It teaches self-discipline and endows the followers of Islam with extra strength, enabling them better to face life's problems and to withstand any tribulation suffered because of their loyalty to the faith. By fasting for a whole month the devout are drawn ever closer to each other and to God. Moreover, by abstaining from food the Muslim learns how it feels to be hungry and will therefore be all the more willing to practise compassion and charity towards those in need — one of the five pillars of Islam.

During the month in which God gave his revelation to Muhammed, Muslims are also expected to dedicate much time to the study of the Quran. Specially pious people will try to read it from cover to cover. Ramadan was also the month in which the battle of Badr was fought. The faithful of Medina defeated the idolatrous forces of Mecca who were invading their city. The victory was a turning point in the history of Islam and its commemoration gives the month even greater meaning and significance for all Muslims.

Id al-Fitr:

The Festival of the Breaking of the Fast

Immediately on the conclusion of Ramadan there commences one of the two major feasts of Islam, appropriately called the Festival of the Breaking of the Fast, *Id al-Fitr* in Arabic. It takes place on the first day of Shawal, the tenth month of the Muslim year.

It is a most joyous occasion, mainly for two reasons. A strenuous period has come to an end and the faithful are sure that, as God has promised, they will be rewarded on the day of judgment for having observed the fast. The moment the new moon is in the sky, indicating the beginning of the feast, people congratulate and wish each other a 'joyful festival'.

Preparations for the holy day begin days beforehand. Houses are decorated and Id greeting cards sent out to members of the family and to friends. Special food is cooked in advance and money is distributed among the poor, lest they miss out on the celebration.

On the day itself, the faithful don new clothes, visit each other and the graves of their loved ones, exchange presents and — aware of their social obligation — give food to the poor. They gather in mosques and in public places for special Id prayers.

Significantly, Islam's prohibition of alcoholic drink does not diminish the genuine happiness that this festival brings to its participants.

Id al-Adha:

The Feast of Sacrifice

The Feast of Sacrifice, *Id al-Adha*, is the second of Islam's most important festivals. It is held on the tenth day of the twelfth month, the month of the Hajj, when Muslims go on pilgrimage to the Holy City of Mecca. To undertake this pilgrimage is the highest ambition in their life. Even those who stay at home join in its celebration, which centres on the sacrifice of an animal.

The sacrifice recalls the dramatic incident in Abraham's life when, according to Muslim tradition, he was about to sacrifice his son Ishmael in obedience to a command from God. At the last moment a divine voice stopped him from slaying his son and directed him to offer a ram in his stead. And this is the message of the festival: like Abraham, every Muslim must be prepared to obey God's wishes and to do so at all costs, no matter how great the sacrifice.

On the morning of the festival Muslims sacrifice an animal, usually a sheep or a goat. Symbolically following Abraham's example, they express their readiness to give their own life whenever God demands.

The meat of the slaughtered animal is divided into three parts. One portion is kept for a family meal, the second is presented to friends and the rest is distributed among the needy or handed to charitable institutions.

Although it is more serious in mood, Id al-Adha shares some customs — such as visiting friends and giving presents — with the more joyous celebration of Id al-Fitr.

Minor Muslim Festivals

*A*dditional festivals throughout the year highlight other significant events in the history of Islam and Muhammed's life.

Muharram:

New Year's Day

*M*uharram is the first month of the Muslim year. Its first day, accordingly, is celebrated as New Year's Day. It is also linked with Muhammed's 'departure' (the *Hijrah*) from Mecca to Medina in AD 622, which is regarded as the most important event in the establishment of Islam and the beginning, the Year One, of the Muslim era.

Rather than an occasion of exuberant festivities and joyous parties, it is a solemn day of introspection on which Muslims renew their resolve to come ever closer to God.

Ashurah

*A*shurah means 'ten'. The festival of Ashurah occurs on the tenth day of Muharram and is a day of voluntary fasting. It is by tradition the anniversary of two important events: Noah's leaving the Ark and Moses' freeing of the Israelites from Pharaoh's bondage.

Shiah Muslims mourn on this day, as it is also the anniversary of the martyrdom of Husein, Muhammed's grandson, at Karbala, Iraq, in AD 680.

The Prophet's Birthday

Muhammed was born on 20 April 570 which, according to the Muslim calendar, is the twelfth day of its third month, Rabi' al-Awal. The founder of Islam, he was, according to Muslim faith, the greatest and last of all prophets. He was 'the seal of prophecy', to whom God revealed the entirety of the Quran — all of its 114 chapters, or *Suras,* as they are called. The day of his birth, therefore, was of paramount importance and its anniversary is an occasion for special celebration.

Gatherings and processions distinguish the day, with the participants sharing traditional sweets and pastries.

The Night of the Ascent

The night of Muhammed's ascent to heaven — on 27 Rajab, the seventh month of the calendar — is celebrated annually. On that night, so tradition has it, Muhammed, guided by the Archangel Gabriel, travelled from Mecca to Jerusalem where he ascended to heaven from a rock. The rock from which he alighted to celestial heights is now venerated in the Mosque of the Rock.

Hindu Celebrations

*H*induism is the native religion of India and its history covers a period of well-nigh five millennia. Its philosophy and teachings are wide-ranging and comprise an infinite variety of ideas, beliefs and rituals. The Rig Veda, one of its ancient holy books, quotes as the fundamental tenet of the faith that 'Truth is One, though sages call it variously'.

Of the many gods worshipped, three are paramount: Brahma, the Creator; Vishnu, the Preserver; and Siva, the Destroyer.

There are many festivals at all times of the year. Some of them are peculiar to specific regions of India. Other feasts are universally observed.

Holi:

The Festival of Colour

Holi is the Hindu festival of spring and usually falls in February or March. It is a happy season that lasts between three and ten days. It is distinguished by colourful floats and exuberant processions. People dance in the streets and light bonfires.

The festival is called after Holika, a she-demon, and one of the conspicuous features of the celebration is the burning of her effigy together with those of other demons. It is meant to symbolise the hoped-for destruction of the powers of evil.

Holi, 'the festival of colour', has acquired this name from the people's practice of squirting coloured water and throwing red powder on each other and passers-by. They do so in recollection of a legend told about the god Krishna as a youth. Krishna is worshipped during Holi. According to the legend the young Krishna was working as a cowherd and amused himself by throwing milk and yellow powder over the maids who were sharing his work. In response, they showered him with red powder.

Janmashtami:

Krishna's Birthday

The Hindu god Vishnu, the Preserver, assumed many forms in order to save the world and its people. Krishna was his eighth

incarnation. Janmashtami, falling during August or September, is the anniversary of his birth. The day is celebrated by the re-enactment of incidents that occurred in the god's early life. Special ceremonies take place in every temple dedicated to him. Their principal feature is the display of Krishna's image as an infant.

The image is bathed in milk mixed with sugar, honey and butter, after which it is laid into a silver cradle, together with toys. At night time the baby is carried through the streets in torchlight processions. As it passes, people hold out their hands, in hopeful expectation that some of the mixture still adhering to the image may drop on them.

Dussehra:

The Festival of Victory

Dussehra, celebrated in the autumn around September or October, is one of the most important Indian festivals. It honours the Divine Mother, the ten-armed goddess Durga, and pays homage to the creative force of the universe. The variety of ways in which this holiday is observed in the various parts of the country is a reflection of the colourful diversity of Hinduism.

The name *Dussehra* merely represents the numeral '10'. This was chosen because it is a ten-day festival. Its main theme is the conquest of evil with the aid of the goddess, who is portrayed in many forms. In West Bengal, for instance, she is represented as destroying a buffalo-headed demon. According to tradition the feast originated in a fearsome battle in which Rama, with the help of Durga, annihilated Ravana, the demon king. Throughout the ten days of the festival,

effigies of Ravana and his evil associates are paraded through the streets. Packed with crackers and explosives, they are finally blown up — just as goodness will in the end vanquish evil.

Dancing, week-long fairs, the sounding of large horns and festive decoration of houses with images of gods, dolls and toys, are some of the many other ways worshippers celebrate. A conspicuous element in the procession held in Mysore is the inclusion of elephants and beautifully ornamented horses.

Diwali:

The Festival of Lights

Diwali occurs in October or November. Based on an enchanting story, this festival of lights has a ceremonial that literally spreads light all over the country. It celebrates the return of a prince to his country after fourteen years of unjust banishment. His people jubilantly welcomed him and made him their king. To mark the occasion and express their joy, they lit lamps everywhere. This is exactly how the festival is now celebrated, with thousands of clay oil lamps illuminating the homes and streets.

Also worshipped during this feast is Lakshmi, the goddess of wealth and prosperity. Her ritual has very practical aspects. To welcome her, homes are spring-cleaned, all damage is repaired, the walls are whitewashed and fireworks set off to scare away evil spirits. It is a special festival for business people. They open up new account books and ask the goddess to bless them with plenty of profit and much success in all their undertakings.

The Sacred Days
of Buddhism

Buddhism dates from the sixth century BC. It was founded by Siddhartha Gautama, son of a powerful ruler in northern India. He was born in about 563 BC and at the age of nineteen he married a princess. Ten years later he abandoned his home, his wife and the child she had borne him to turn his back on the world of pleasure and become an ascetic and a wandering monk. When he was thirty-five years old, he was meditating under a banyan tree one day, when enlightenment came to him: 'Then I did become certain that I had attained the full knowledge of highest wisdom in heaven and on earth'. Siddhartha had become the 'Enlightened One', the 'Buddha', by which name he has been known ever since.

Buddha concentrated on the problem of suffering that haunts man and the entire world. His final teaching was aimed at lessening pain of any kind and striving for the supreme goal of all existence, the stage of Nirvana. It is a term which is untranslatable but which refers to the cessation of all desire, the extinction of greed, anger and delusion, and the union with ultimate reality. To reach this goal man had to follow 'the noble eightfold path' of: (1) Right Knowledge; (2) Right Intention; (3) Right Speech; (4) Right Action; (5) Right Means of Livelihood; (6) Right Effort; (7) Right Thought; and (8) Right Concentration.

The faith he taught eventually divided into two branches: the 'Southern School' (known as Theravada Buddhism), which is specifically followed in Sri Lanka, Myanmar (formerly Burma) and Thailand; and the 'Northern School' (designated Mahayana Buddhism), which is practised in China and Japan. Whilst the former school regards Buddha as an enlightened teacher, the latter sees him as a divine being. Buddhist holidays vary in different places, but they also overlap.

Wesak:

A Threefold Anniversary

As a threefold anniversary — of Buddha's birth, enlightenment and death — Wesak is the most sacred Buddhist festival. The name is merely the Singhalese description of this lunar month. Held

at the time of the full moon mostly in April or May, it is celebrated by the entire Buddhist world.

Homes and streets are decorated and gifts distributed among both monks and the poor. Some faithful even open up free eating places on roadsides, entertaining anyone who passes by. In other regions, special credit is given to those who release caged birds.

Khao Phansa:
The Buddhist Lent

The Buddhist Lent — lasting a full three months — falls during the rainy season, beginning in July. During that time no wedding is solemnised or other festivity celebrated. Offerings are presented to the monks who stay in retreat throughout the whole period, joined by laymen anxious to be taught by them.

It is believed that this extensive season of retreat dates back to Buddha's time, when the rains made it impossible for him and his disciples to proceed on their travels and spread their message. Yet another reason given for the monks staying inside their monasteries is their determination not to break one of Buddhism's principals: not to do harm to or cause the death of even the least of creatures. At this season, because of the wet, swarms of insects fill the air. The monks could easily cause their death by either inadvertently swallowing or inhaling them or by stepping on them while walking about outside.

The Buddhist New Year

The celebration of the Buddhist New Year is an occasion of great joy. As Hindus do during Holi, people in their exuberance squirt water on whomever they meet in the streets, regardless of whether it is a friend or a stranger. Homage is paid to the various statues of the Buddha, which are ceremoniously bathed.

The Northern School

The festivals of Mahayana Buddhism, like those of Theravada Buddhism, include the celebration of Buddha's birth, enlightenment and death. However, adherents of Mahayana Buddhism also celebrate the birthdays of reincarnated Buddhas and of the founders of other schools.

Whenever possible holy days are kept at the time of the full moon. A particular feast is set aside to show concern for dead souls, and features of this have been adopted in the Chinese 'Festival of Hungry Ghosts'.

Chinese Festivals

An abundance of celebrations is part of Chinese culture. With their unique talent for compromise, the Chinese have been able to combine in their observances elements of Confucianism, Buddhism and Taoism. Respectfully and tolerantly, they subscribe to them all, even though aspects of them have been secularised. A Chinese saying compares the three traditions to the three legs of a tripod: they support the entire structure of their life, and by ignoring even one of them, the structure would falter, and even collapse.

The most important Chinese festival is the Chinese New Year. Because it is observed widely throughout the world — and acknowledged by many non-Chinese people — it is described in detail in the 'Calendar Year' section of the book under 'January'.

The Feast of Lanterns

Ranking in importance and splendour next to — and following in the calendar soon after — the celebration of the New Year, is the Feast of Lanterns. It is held on the fifteenth day of the first lunar month, the 'First Full Moon'.

Originally a seasonal event, it was concerned with the rebirth of nature after the cold of winter. The ritual of the lanterns was intended to increase the light and warmth of the sun!

Soon people discovered the beauty of the lanterns, apart from any cosmic influence they might exert. So they added ever more lamps and the festival assumed a most lavish scale. Lanterns are hung up both inside and outside the homes, in the streets and all public places — brightly illuminating the night. Fire crackers are set off and, as at all Chinese festivals, the people consume an abundance of food and drink.

The Dragon Boat Festival

The Dragon Boat Festival is the biggest summer event in the Chinese calendar. It is celebrated by boat races. The boats, painted in bright red, are decorated at their prow with a dragon's head, which explains the name of the festival.

A tragic incident in the third century BC is said to have been responsible for the introduction of the festival. In 285 BC Chu Yuan, a member of a noble family and a great poet and patriot of the Chu dynasty, roused his king's anger by fearlessly denouncing him for his injustice and corruption. As a punishment, he was exiled to Hunan. As the years passed he longed more and more for his home and loved ones. Utterly depressed, he decided to end his life. On the fifth day of the fifth moon in 278 BC, he threw himself into the Milo River. Fishermen who witnessed his suicide attempt immediately tried to save him from drowning or being devoured by man-eating fish that infested

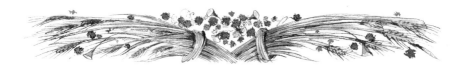

the waters. They raced their boats towards him and, to divert the fish from the drowning man, tossed bits of food to them. However, they did not succeed. Their vain attempts are re-enacted annually by the dragon boat races and the throwing of rice into the water. Yet another feature of the festival — now so far removed from the harrowing event — is the eating of rice dumplings!

Because it is held on the fifth day of the fifth lunar month — supposedly the anniversary of Chu Yuan's death — the day is also known as the 'Double Five Festival'.

The Feast of the Hungry Ghosts

Living people who are neglected are usually powerless to make others remember and help them. But not so, according to Chinese belief, the souls of the dead, particularly during the seventh lunar month when, temporarily released from the netherworld, they wander the earth in search of affection. They are known as the hungry ghosts because of their hunger for recognition and care.

Their number is increased by the souls of people who died unnatural deaths — who were drowned or murdered, or just disappeared from the earth without being given a proper burial place which their families could visit in order to pay them respect. Other such 'hungry ghosts' that are abroad during this month are the spirits of people whose families had either died out or who showed no concern for their welfare in the beyond. Bereft of comfort, they feel abandoned and, lacking ancestral worship, may turn malignant and become powerful threats to the living.

The Festival of the Hungry Ghosts, held on the fifteenth day of this fateful month, is particularly dedicated to these earthbound spirits. Its purpose is to make them feel welcome and to satisfy their spiritual hunger. This will placate any possible anger they might have and gain their gratitude.

In the sacred ritual of that day, the spirits are offered joss sticks, food and gifts. The gifts, made of paper, represent objects with which they were familiar while on earth and are intended to make them feel at home. Paper money is burnt on their behalf, to pay for their expenses in the netherworld. Fires, lit during the night on roadsides, street corners and in temples, serve both as a guide to the hungry ghosts and as a gesture of welcome.

In some regions, special performances are staged for the entertainment of the ghosts on their eerie visit, in the hope that these will make them forget their grudges and encourage them to return to their abode with a feeling of acceptance. Their hunger allayed, at last they will have found peace and rest.

The Moon Festival

The Chinese celebrate the Moon Festival by treating their family and friends with moon cakes, so called because of their round shape. It is a joyous occasion indeed with the festive gatherings and unique gifts dating back to a significant historic occasion. There are also cosmic explanations of its origins.

It is related that during the Yuan dynasty in the fourteenth

century Mongols ruled the people with an iron hand, taking away from them all their freedom. Determined to throw off the yoke, a resistance movement came into existence. It chose the most brilliant night of the year — the fifteenth night of the eighth month according to the lunar calendar — to stage a rebellion.

However, as they were constantly watched by guards who were billeted in their homes, the plotters had to be very careful to avoid detection of their intended uprising. To coordinate the rebellion which they had fixed for the stroke of midnight, they passed on their message on scraps of paper which they hid in moon cakes and sent all over the city to their fellow conspirators.

Their plan succeeded, and this early victory of democracy over despotism is recalled at the Moon Festival with feasting and rejoicing. It is celebrated on the anniversary of the deliverance.

According to the cosmic explanation the Chinese, early on, were convinced that the destiny of the world was determined largely by lunar power. It is no wonder, then, that they dedicated a special festival to the moon, to be held at the very time when it was believed to be at its brightest. According to this tradition, the moon cakes were first baked with magical intent, to ensure that the heavenly body would bestow its blessing on the universe and, after periods of waning, would increase again to its full strength.

Delicious in taste, the brown pastry cakes are filled with a paste made mainly of sweet beans and ground lotus seeds. Significantly, they are embossed with the emblem of the lunar god. Some of the moon cakes are offered to the silver disc in the sky, 'to promote harmony between man and moon'. Others are sent as gifts to neighbours and friends, 'to promote a close relationship between man and man'.

Japanese
Celebrations

Japan is a country of festivals. No cost is spared and much time is spent in their celebration. Some are held nationwide, while others, though centred on local shrines, attract crowds from all over Japan.

Shrine festivals, in particular, are distinguished by processions of floats. The number and magnificence of these floats give an indication of how highly rated a particular festival is. Some of the floats are more than a hundred years old, of enormous size and are, indeed, outstanding works of art.

The reasons for the celebrations are varied. Some are linked with legendary or historic figures of the distant past while others focus on present-day life and the needs of the people, or show concern for the future.

The Japanese word for 'festival' is Matsuri, and it often features in the names of individual festivals. Originally it meant 'worship' or 'service'.

Hadaka Matsuri:
The 'Naked Festival'

*C*elebrated around the time of the (old lunar) New Year is Hadaka Matsuri, the 'Naked Festival'. It is so called because the young men who participate in its rituals do so almost naked. All they wear are white loin cloths and white or coloured headbands.

They wrestle with each other according to rules which may differ from district to district. The ritual 'match' is not an ordinary sporting event, nor is it intended as entertainment. It has deep religious significance. It is believed magically to rid the participants, and the country, of all bad luck, ill health and impurity, thereby ensuring a year of good fortune.

The Festival of Bonten:
The Story of a Divine Conductor

*T*he Festival of Bonten is also held early in the year — in the middle of February — when harsh winter prevails in the northern region. It received its name from the huge heavy wooden poles which play a central role in its ritual.

The basis of the celebration is the desire that heavenly blessing should descend to earth to help people overcome the hardships of winter and to bring a rich harvest and prosperity to the land.

In an ancient ritual the god was provided, at least symbolically, with a ladder that linked heaven and earth and that made it easier for him to descend from his celestial heights. This was the function of a huge pole, the Bonten, set up in the god's shrine. It was like a conductor — attracting and guiding divine power.

Groups of up to twenty young men select and fashion their individual pole. They decorate it with colourful bunting and a crown of highly artistic design. In exciting competition, the teams then race to the shrine each carrying its Bonten. Whoever arrives first has the privilege of having it erected in the sanctuary!

Not surprisingly, this contest makes for a joyful and exuberant festival — rendering a religious occasion a truly enjoyable and vital experience.

Yuki Matsuri:
The Snow Festival

The Snow Festival, Yuki Matsuri, is modern in its origin and devoid of any religious tradition. It began as recently as 1950, and is held during the first weekend of February in the city of Sapporo on the island of Hokkaido. As its name suggests, it centres on the joys of winter and is designed to foster a specific type of art that only this season can provide: sculptures made of ice and snow.

The main feature of its celebration, therefore, is a competition involving such sculptures, with a different theme chosen every year. Sculptures may vary from life-sized figures from classical Greek mythology to intricate representations of everyday objects.

The Gion Festival:
It All Started in an Epidemic

*S*ickness has always haunted mankind, especially when it seemed beyond its power to subdue. People then realised that only divine intervention could halt it. The celebration of the Gion Festival originated in one instance of this realisation.

A devastating epidemic struck Kyoto in AD 869. Hundreds of citizens fell victim to it. It became obvious that only some supernatural means could stop the disease, so a strange ritual was devised. The chief priest of the Gion Shrine gathered sixty-six spears, each representing one of the provinces of Japan. He mounted them on a portable shrine. He transported this — spears and all — to the emperor's garden and immersed it in a sacred pond. He was convinced that, thus purified, the spears would chase away the evil spirits of sickness.

Instantly, the plague stopped. In acknowledgment of the god's help, the priest carried the sacred implements of the shrine through the streets of Kyoto, dramatically bringing home to the people the fact that only divine help had saved their city.

His show of gratitude, re-enacted every year, developed into the spectacular festival that now occupies the entire month of July. No longer related to sickness and its miraculous cure, it recalls and, honours a rich variety of figures and events of the Japanese past. Gion Matsuri, indeed, is not only one of the major festivals that centres on Kyoto — Japan's capital for more than a thousand years — but is also one of the most resplendent celebrations in the country.

Its outstanding feature is a spectacular procession of picturesque floats. Each is named after the scene it depicts. Some of the floats weigh up to ten tons and tower to a height of sixty-five feet (20 m). They are pulled by large teams of up to twenty people. Residents who live along the route of the pageant open the doors of their homes as it passes to display some of their own precious possessions — usually antique folding screens.

Throughout the festival lanterns illuminate the streets and all the people join happily in the celebrations.

The Bon Festival :

When the Dead Visit the Living

The fifteenth of July is the Japanese 'Memorial Day', known as the Bon Festival. Services in honour of ancestors, dead relatives and friends are held at temples and in private homes. The souls of the dead are believed to revisit their former abode on that day. Everything possible is done to extend to them a worthy welcome. To help them

find their way more easily, ornate lanterns, made of white paper, are hung up.

Food prepared for the nourishment of the souls is placed on special trays which are kept for this purpose. The food is reserved for the dead alone. Even if, after the soul's departure, it appears undiminished, it is still believed that — invisibly and unnoticed — the dead have partaken of it. At the conclusion of the feast the food, untouched by the living, will be tossed into the river or sea.

The origin of the festival and its custom are explained by a legend. A man, anxious to find out how his dead parents were faring in the world beyond, was granted a vision. He was horrified to see his mother suffering agonies of hunger. To stop her anguish, he immediately prepared a large bowl of food for her. But each time she was about to eat from it, the food turned into flames. Desperate, the son consulted a priest. He was told that his mother was being punished for sins she had committed while on earth.

Divine mercy alone could save her, and this could be obtained only by an intense effort of prayer, undertaken by a gathering of sacred men. The son lost no time in contacting numerous priests. Providing them with a large quantity of food, he implored them, for his mother's salvation, to hold a joint prayer meeting. They did so. His mother's trespasses were forgiven and she no longer had to suffer starvation.

The date of the worship and of the mother's release from hunger, was the fifteenth day of the seventh month. Ever since, it has been remembered by the Bon Festival with its welcome to the visiting spirits and the special food offered them.

Bon is the Japanese word for a 'tray' or 'bowl' (as used in *bonsai*

which means 'tray planting'). Obviously, the festival was so named because of the trays filled with food, which are its most conspicuous feature.

The Nebuta Festival:

A Festival to Ward off Sleep

The Japanese are renowned for their innate industriousness. Few people, therefore, would regard it necessary for them to reserve an entire day (in the first week of August) to invoke the help of supernatural powers to prevent them going slack in their work. But this was the original meaning and purpose of the Nebuta Festival. Held prior to the beginning of the rice crop, it was intended to ward off sleepiness during the gathering of the grain.

On all other festive occasions, the floats used are dismantled at the end of the feast and their parts are carefully stored away to be reassembled in the following year. Not so at the *Nebuta* festival. On its conclusion, the floats are cast into the river, in the hope that its waters will carry them out to sea and, with them, take away the spirit of sleep. This final ceremony became known as 'the washing away [of] sleep'.

Another explanation traces the origin of the feast to a ninth-century rebellion in the far-off northernmost part of Honshu. The region was isolated from the imperial centre and the number of troops stationed there was insufficient to quell the uprising. So the emperor employed a ruse. He had dummy figures of soldiers placed along a line. Unaware that these were not real, the rebels felt greatly outnumbered, and surrendered. In commemoration of this bloodless victory

processions are held every year on its anniversary. They include figures of colossal size, carried on men's shoulders or on carts. Made of papier-mâché on a framework of bamboo and wire, the giant dolls (called *Nebuta*) measure up to sixty-five feet (20 m) in width and thirty-five feet (10.5 m) in height.

Kurama No-Hi-Matsuri:

The Fire Festival of Kurama

The district of Kyoto can pride itself on yet another auspicious celebration, the Fire Festival of Kurama, which is held on 22 October. People of all ages join in a solemn procession, carrying lighted grass torches. The grass, cut five months earlier, is left to dry in preparation for this occasion. Bonfires, spaced at regular intervals on either side of the parade's route, add further to the splendour and brightness of the spectacle.

It was not to worship the forces of fire, however, that the festival was introduced, but in honour of the annual visit of the gods and the spirits. Initially, therefore, the torches and bonfires were merely a means to an end. They were lit to invite and welcome the heavenly guests and to light up their path on their way from their celestial abode to earth!

As time passed, people forgot the original function of the fires and lit them, not for the sake of the gods and the spirits, but simply for their own enjoyment. Soon, however, the practice took on a new religious significance. As they carefully watched the fires, people interpreted the height to which they rose and the direction in which the smoke drifted as divine predictions of their future and fortunes.

The Seven-Day Week

Originally, days did not have individual names and weeks did not exist. The smallest unit in the calendar was the month. When life became more complex the convenience of shorter units of time became obvious, and the week was invented.

At first its length varied from one culture to another, from a mere four up to ten days. It was usually the interval between market days or days that were regarded as specially sacred.

The modern seven-day week comes from ancient Babylonia. Babylonian astronomers — among the first in the world — had identified in the sky what they called the seven 'planets'. They believed these to be divine celestial bodies which guarded and influenced life. Seven thus became a holy number to them, symbolic of completion. And seven days completed the week!

The Hebrews acquired the seven-day week from the Babylonians. No record has done more for its adoption than the biblical story of Genesis which tells how, after six days of creation, God rested from his work on the seventh day — ever since known as the Sabbath.

The Hebrews did not give individual names to the seven days of

their week. They merely counted the position of each after the Sabbath, calling Wednesday, for instance, 'the third day', and Thursday 'the fourth'.

The Egyptians introduced the practice of calling days by particular names. They chose for them the names of the seven planets, in which they included the sun and the moon.

The Romans followed the Egyptian example and, when they invaded and occupied northern Europe, they introduced their names of the days. The Roman system was never abandoned, although the Anglo-Saxons soon replaced most of the Roman divinities with the names of equivalent Norse gods.

The days of the week thus have their origins in ancient myth and astronomy. Like the names of the months, they have remained unchanged over many centuries and no day passes by without modern man paying unconscious tribute to a figure or power in which he no longer believes.

The Names of the Days

SUNDAY recalls the early worship of the sun. It was only in the fourth century that the Church declared it a holy day. As it was the day of Christ's resurrection it was to replace the celebration of the Jewish Sabbath.

MONDAY is the moon's day. It is dedicated to the lunar deity, whose memory is also perpetuated in the word 'month', which is derived from 'moon'.

TUESDAY honours Tiu or Tiw, the Norse god of war. He corresponds to the Roman Mars who, faring rather better, is commemorated by an entire month — the month of March.

WEDNESDAY is Wodan's day. Its name offers an interesting example of the phenomenon of metathesis — the transposition in the order of letters. Strictly, the day should be known as 'Wedensday'. Woden, better known as Odin, was the god of storms. He welcomed brave warriors to Valhalla and rewarded their valour by providing them with the pleasure they most desired while on earth. He was the father of Thor and husband of Frigga.

THURSDAY is Thor's day. The oldest son of Odin and Frigga, he was the Norse god of thunder and lightning. Appropriately, he is portrayed with a hammer and an iron glove, the latter enabling him so much more easily to throw his bolts. He was also worshipped as the god who brought good luck and, accordingly, his images were carved on houses and ships.

FRIDAY is called after Frigga, the Norse goddess of love, marriage and fertility and counterpart of the Roman Venus. The only female deity in the sequence of days, she was chosen, it has been said, mainly to pacify her feelings of neglect. After all, as the preceding days bore the names of her husband and her son, it seemed only reasonable to include her too.

SATURDAY is the day of Saturn, the Roman god of sowing who is commemorated as well in the festival of the Saturnalia. His presence in the nomenclature of days links the worship of a planet to that of the sun and moon.

Friday the 13th

riday the 13th has become an ominous day because of its association, both in legend and in history, with great misfortune. Jesus was crucified on Friday. Tradition has it, too, that Adam and Eve ate of the forbidden fruit and were expelled from the Garden of Eden on a Friday. Other disastrous biblical events alleged to have occurred on Friday were Cain's murder of Abel and the confusion of tongues at Babel, which resulted in people's being scattered all over the world.

Jesus' death on a Friday also made people think that on that day the powers of evil were at their very height. It was, therefore, the most sinister day of the week, on which people were exposed to greater risks than on any other day.

That thirteen is an unlucky number is a deeply rooted notion, or superstition, that goes back to early classical times. Greek philosophers taught that numbers dominated life. They gave each number a specific property that could bring good fortune, or bad luck.

Of all numbers, thirteen stood out as the most ominous. Indivisible, it stood all on its own, seemingly shunning other numbers and being shunned by them.

Traditionally, indeed, thirteen has proved an unlucky number. At the Last Supper, Jesus and the twelve Apostles made up a company of thirteen, a fact that was interpreted as influencing the subsequent course of events and to have resulted in the crucifixion.

If it happens that the thirteenth day of the month falls on a Friday, the evil associated with both the number and the day is compounded.

INDEX